FUTURE PROOFED

How to Navigate Disruptive Change, Find Calm in Chaos, And Succeed in Work & Life

Natalia Peart, PhD

SB

FutureProofed:
How to Navigate Disruptive Change, Find Calm in Chaos, and Succeed in Work & Life
Copyright © 2019 by Natalia Peart, PhD

This is a work of creative nonfiction. The events herein are portrayed to the best of the author's memory. While all the stories in this book are true, some names and identifying details may have been changed to protect the privacy of the people involved.

Scrivener Books
info@scrivenerbooks.com
USA

Editorial work and production management by Eschler Editing
Cover design by Zeljka Kojic & Mitch Chandler, Push Creative
Interior illustrations by Michelle Nelson
Interior print design and layout by Dayna Linton, Day Agency
eBook formatting by Dayna Linton, Day Agency

Library of Congress Control Number: Pending

ISBN: 978-1-949165-10-4 (Paperback)
ISBN: 978-0-463029-78-7 (e-Book)

First Edition: 2019

10 9 8 7 6 5 4 3 2 1

Printed in the USA

SB

TABLE OF CONTENTS

FUTURE
PROOFED

THE ROAD TO SUCCESS IS ON PERMANENT DETOUR

⟨ THE BIG SHIFT ⟩

The World Has Changed

WE'VE BEEN THROUGH PERIODS of change before, but this time it feels different. Our lives have been profoundly altered by the recent economic upheaval, disruptive technology, and accelerating speed of change, not to mention our more globalized and networked world. These seismic shifts have brought both enormous opportunities and colossal challenges. It isn't just the fact that we're experiencing these changes that leaves us so unsettled; it's also the incredible and increasing rate of these changes that's leaving us feeling imbalanced.

And right now we're anxious.

As a nation, we're more divided than ever. Deepening political, economic, and social unrest has moved us into living in prolonged crisis mode. Crisis isn't merely the lead headline in our news anymore; it's the backdrop and filter for our lives. Anxiety is on the rise. And when you add worry over other challenges like our crushing student debt or rising health-care costs to the other big world shifts and deep divisions, it is no wonder we find ourselves beyond our ability to cope.

The World of Work Has Changed

ANOTHER SHIFT IN OUR world has been the transformation of how we must now think about our careers. We all know the old model of lifetime employment in exchange for lifetime loyalty has vanished; instead, we now have a short-term agreement that is constantly up for renewal and renegotiation. Consequently, over the last several decades, we've seen the death of the lifelong job and the creation of more independent ways of working—a freelance economy.

While this trend happened over time, we paid greater attention to it when the 2008 financial crisis forced millions of us out of our "secure" jobs—millions of us who were then forced to seek other forms of employment, full-time or otherwise, that allowed us to take the future into our hands and regain control. This move toward embracing our freelance economy became a necessity for some because of outsourced jobs; for others, it signaled a way to take advantage of the greater opportunities a globalized economy and rapid technological advances ushered in.

What We Want from the World Has Changed

A THIRD BIG SHIFT that has occurred in the midst of our greater opportunities and the constant chaos of our lives is a shift in how we define success. It used to be we viewed success mostly through the narrow lens of financial wealth and how high we rose in position and power.

This view of success forced us to commit more and more of ourselves to climbing the career ladder. Missing from this old model of success, though, was the reality that climbing to higher leadership positions with no changes in home, childcare, structural, or systemic supports made the climb virtually out of reach for far too many who wanted it. We were also seeing high burnout rates for both women and men who were emptying themselves to succeed.

Also missing from this old model was our growing desire to define success beyond position and power. After all the climbing and all the sacrifice, many who were successful were still left asking themselves "Is this all there is?" That's because we no longer want only material success; we also want meaningful lives. And in order to live meaningfully, we want to do work that matters to us. We no longer want to separate who we are from what we do. Instead, we want our work to be an expression of who we are, and we want to be fully engaged in our lives.

Something else was missing from our old paradigm, and it has become especially important in this time of constant uncertainty. We want not only success but the peace of mind that comes from knowing that regardless of whatever change or crisis is just around the corner, we are prepared to withstand it and still maintain control over our lives. What we want is not to just survive, but to thrive in the face of this constant change and disruption.

THE GAP

IF WE STOP FOR moment to think about the effect of all these big shifts collectively on our lives, it's clear these changes are greater than anything we have ever experienced—both as individuals and as a nation.

But the big problem we now also face is the reason I've written this book:

While the times have changed dramatically, we do not have new rules for how to succeed in our new world.

Our old, familiar blueprint for success was based on the world we used to live in: go to school, get a good job, climb the career ladder, work forty hours a week for forty years, retire, and live off 40 percent of what you earned. Irrespective of its flaws and shortcomings, that old path to success is on permanent detour. But here's the problem: we lack a structured way to think about and navigate the *new* path that is in tune with our current needs and how we now define success.

The fact that we have not yet closed this gap is troubling but not too surprising. That's because the places where we would have expected to learn these new navigational skills have just not kept pace.

For example, our educational system was built for a different time. It teaches us how to study for the A and how to be successful in a twentieth-century world, not how to prepare for success in a twenty-first-century economy.

Career development through our employers is now much more limited than it used to be. With the employer-employee pact now broken, employers no longer invest as much in career development because their employees are not expected to stay as long. Why make a financial and resource investment in developing someone who will just take that training somewhere else?

Personal development tends to view our challenges as mostly a motivational problem. But for most people, this problem is not motivational; it is informational and directional. People don't know the new path or how to navigate it in response to our changing times.

⟨ THE WAY FORWARD ⟩

WE SIMPLY CAN'T DO more of what we already know: the old ways of thinking, working, and living are just not enough anymore. What we need is to shift our paradigm—our lens and our perspective—to open us to the new paths, key skills, mindsets, and habits that help us thrive in today's world.

Whether you are looking to invent or reinvent yourself in the face of these unpredictable times, trying to change careers, wanting to advance in your organization, trying to start a new business, or needing to make a personal transition, you now need to know how to:

- Navigate the new road we all must travel.
- Build career confidence, whether you're working for yourself or for someone else, by shifting from just finding your next job to creating a playbook and system for your success.
- Achieve peace of mind by increasing your own financial safety and security.
- Master the one constant in life—change—by building the mental fitness you need to thrive regardless of what's happening around you.
- Develop a success lifestyle by effectively using your time, energy, and attention to live a life that is satisfying and meaningful to you.
- Leverage your success to impact our world.

This book is not about where to find your next job. It is about finding your place amid constant change and uncertainty. It is your guide to navigating life in an ever-changing landscape and taking some power and control back into your own hands. This book is about creating a new way forward so that even in the midst of turbulence, you can find higher ground and you can also make a difference in the world around you.

PRESENT TENSE

As a psychologist and personal and business consultant, I have seen first-hand the impact of constant and disruptive change on individuals and organizations. As you journey through this book, you will learn the strategies that will help you create a new way forward and find clarity even in the midst of turbulence. You'll be going on another kind of journey, too—one where you join five travelers and their guide, Nancy, on a life-changing journey of their own. These travelers are an amalgamation of the people that I have helped over the years find their new way forward. So, sit back and prepare for the journey of your life.

IT SEEMED LIKE ANY other Friday. Gina gathered with her closest friends after work at her studio apartment, as she often did. It was their time to get together after the long week and to decide their plans for the rest of the evening and weekend. But this Friday was different. Gina was eagerly anticipating leaving early tomorrow morning for a trip that promised to be an adventure like no other, and she was excited as she told her friends about it.

In another city one thousand miles away, Roberta was excited but also worried as she talked about the trip with her husband and two young sons as they ate dinner that night. She worried that maybe this wasn't the right time for the trip, but her family encouraged her not to back out as she had done in the past. After dinner, she helped the boys with their projects and checked in on her mother, who lived nearby, before she started packing for the weekend.

———

Shelly just got off the phone with her daughter, a college freshman. Shelly had told her how excited she was that she was finally taking this trip for herself. She'd gone on a few expeditions in the past, but always with work teams. This was the first time Shelly would be doing anything like this on her own. She also told her daughter that while she had no idea what the weekend had in store, she was ready to do something for herself and to stick with it.

———

Bobby had never done anything like this. When he called his parents to tell them he was leaving, they naturally had lots of questions about what the trip was going to be like. Bobby normally loved to play it safe and would be on top of all the details and then some, but this time he had no idea what was going to be happening. It was hard to explain to his parents why he felt he needed to go, and he didn't sleep that night because of his nervous anticipation.

———

Mark thought about all that was riding on this trip as he packed. Like Bobby, he didn't know what the expedition was going to be, but he did know he was at a crossroads in his life. His daughters were the ones who'd told him about the trip. He'd never even considered something like this before, but he hoped it could help him get his life back on track.

———

THE NEXT MORNING, THEY'D each traded the sounds and sights of the city for rustic cabins, red-rock mountains, hiking trails, and rivers—all right outside their back door. Once they settled in, the five strangers met for the first time in the main cabin area. As they took some time to greet each other informally, they learned they all came from different parts of the country. Nancy, their instructor and guide, welcomed them, told them a bit about herself, and asked each of them to introduce themselves to the group.

Roberta started.

"I'm Roberta, and I came because I'm burned out. I have an okay job working in HR; I like my job, but I don't love it. I'm able to make my job sound a lot better than it feels to me. I'm married, and I have a ten-year-old and twelve-year-old who have been my life since the day they were born. I now help take care of my mother in addition to helping my husband through his recent career ups and downs. I see my friends less and less because we're all busy. What I know is that right now I feel like I'm just going through the motions. Every day I go through my list of obligations, my must-dos. I feel like every step of the way, I made lots of reasonable choices. But I don't know—maybe I've made too many compromises, because the problem is, I just don't know what it all adds up to. I feel like I've run myself ragged but not come even close to fulfilling my potential. The truth is, I feel empty inside, like I'm sleepwalking, but now it feels better not to be awake because the light inside is gone. I'm here because I don't know what my life adds up to, and I'm just too tired to figure it out."

Bobby went next.

"I'm Bobby, and I'm a computer programmer. I feel fortunate to have had a good job right out of college, but five years into it I feel like it's time to move on. I feel I have more to offer. The fact that I make decent money, at least enough to cover my expenses and to help pay back my student loans, should be enough, right? But it's not. I saw so many people with good jobs lose so much during the recession, and now I see so many people like me with a degree and lots of student debt who are not really able to move forward. I thought good grades and a degree were going to be enough. I feel educated but not prepared, and it's so unsettling. I've outgrown my job, the way I am living, and even where I'm living, but I don't feel like I know how to move forward or prepare for what may be around the next corner. I'm here because I'm school successful but can't figure out how to be life successful, and it's time for me to figure it out."

Gina was the next to take the floor.

"I'm Gina, and I graduated college with a degree in journalism. I've spent most of my time since college piecing together lots of different jobs just so I can make sure I cover my rent, food, and transportation costs, not to mention my heavy student-loan debt. My biggest problem isn't getting a job—it's securing a good job that allows me to launch my career, and my life, in a way that covers my bills and feels meaningful to me. I'm not where I want to be in life. I feel like I'm flailing, and I'm worried. I'm worried I won't be able to afford my studio apartment and that at some point I may have to move back home. My parents help me out from time to time, and I have to admit I feel like I'm waiting for my life to start. I'm tired of working dead-end jobs and would love to do something that really matters to me. I'm a writer, but I'm stuck with the feeling that I'll never find anything more than a job. I look at others who graduated with me, and I have to admit I'm jealous. I don't envy their actual jobs, but they don't seem to be spinning in circles like I seem to be doing every day. I feel lost trying to make sense of it all."

Having had time to think about what she was going to say, Shelly went next.

"I'm Shelly, and I'm a marketing executive. From the outside, my life looks pretty good. Actually, it looks really good. I've always been on the fast track, the superstar at work, and rewarded for that. I've stayed focused and pushed everything out of the way today so I could live for tomorrow—that next reward, that next promotion. I came here today because I want to know what's wrong with me—because after all the studying, training, pain, sacrifice, and missed family and school events, where is the happiness that was supposed to come along as part of the success package? Instead, I feel there is so much more inside me that I know I'm supposed to be doing but I'm not. Every day I'm more aware of time running out. Every day wasted doing what I'm doing right now feels like it's sucking the life out of me, but the idea of starting over to live my dreams terrifies me. I think I'm afraid to step out of what has made me successful so far because of the paycheck and the lifestyle I've built around it. All for something that is not certain. I feel like I've made the wrong choices in my life, and I fear that this is it for me."

Mark wrapped up the discussion with his introduction.

"I'm Mark, and I teach part-time at my local college. I used to be an operations manager in a company that had huge layoffs right after the recession, and it took me awhile to secure another position. I feel like a used-to-have. My wife and I used to have a home but lost it to foreclosure. I have two kids in college we help, so we live paycheck to paycheck. Everyone pitches in, and I know I am supposed to feel grateful that no one has gotten too sick or had any major emergencies because we just couldn't pay for something like that. I used to be able to take care of myself no matter what, and my family could depend on me. So to struggle financially this way is painful. I used to have goals, but not anymore. My wife and I argue all the time, and she says I should help her more around the house. Maybe she's right, but to do so would be to admit I've failed at the one thing I'm supposed to do—provide. I'm here because, for the first time in my life, I'm scared."

By this time, the people in the room almost seemed to have forgotten Nancy was there. They just kept talking and sharing more about what brought them there. As they got to know one another, Nancy put some paper up on the wall and gave them two questions to consider. The first was *Why are you here now? Why now?* The second question was *What do you want from this journey?* Nancy provided lots of sticky notes so the group members could write as many responses as they wanted. Here's what they said:

⟨ WHY NOW? ⟩

- I thought my education would prepare me for life, but it didn't.
- I don't feel like I've turned into the person I thought I would be or have the life I expected to have.
- I feel vulnerable to the next crisis—it's really unsettling.
- I feel off track, and I keep thinking I must've done something really wrong because I've no idea how I ended up here.
- This is not where I thought I would be at this point in my life.
- Life feels so unpredictable, and I am anxious about my future.
- I'm living an empty life without purpose or passion.
- Life is passing me by; I can't get my life right.
- I'm treading water financially.
- We were told if we followed the rules, we would be okay. It didn't work out like that.

- I feel like I am still scrambling at forty, just like I was in my twenties.
- It seems I should love my life, but every day I am more aware of how I am living in fear. I can't ignore it anymore.
- I'm not sure how to create the future I want.
- I'm in survival mode and on the hamster wheel. I don't see the payoff at all.
- I have a good education, but it still feels harder to get ahead. Not sure what to do.
- My daughter is in school, and I have no idea what to tell her about how to prepare.

WHAT DO YOU WANT FROM THIS JOURNEY?

- I want to know how to be successful despite the constant change in life.
- I want more control over my life.
- I want peace of mind that I can weather a storm.
- I want to know how to take advantage of opportunity.
- I want to be on a path that restores hope.
- I just want to feel like one thing in my life is certain.
- I want to work for a purpose, not just a paycheck.
- I want to do something that really matters to me.
- I used to have fire, and I want it back.
- I want to not feel so vulnerable.
- I want to know how to find my way in this new world.
- I want the safety and security I've worked so hard to build up, and I want to feel as though I have fulfilled my potential.
- I want to not let go of my dreams.

- I want to feel fulfilled.
- I am searching for a bigger vision for my life—not merely exist.

To get where we've never been, we need to do what we've never done.

—Unknown

"As you all know from your invitation, this is a come-as-you-are journey," Nancy said. "I asked you not to pack anything special because everything you need is here. But this is not going to be your typical retreat. Each day, we are going someplace you have never been, and we will be doing what you've never done. This journey we're about to take is for you if you are ready to think about the way you shape both your career and life in a very different way. It is for you if you are looking to find solutions in the midst of what feels like chaos and confusion."

"This journey is about giving you choices so you can control your destiny. But to get to where you want, you can no longer play by the same rules of success you're used to playing by, and here's why: The world has changed, which means we live in a time of constant change and greater uncertainty. The world of work has changed because we've seen the death of the job for life and the rise of more independent ways of working. And what we want from the world has changed, so the narrow way we used to think about success no longer satisfies."

The Journey Ahead

Nancy then gave a brief overview of the five journeys the group would be taking. "For our first journey, we are going to discover a new blueprint for success and *FutureProofing*. Our second journey will take us from just knowing how to find a job to learning a whole new strategy for creating a playbook and system for success. All along the way, we are going to develop the skills to be *FutureProofed* so we can create our own financial safety and security. Our third journey will be building the mental fitness we need to not just survive but thrive regardless of what is happening around us. The fourth will teach us to create a success lifestyle by effectively using our resources, time, energy, and attention to live in a way that is most satisfying to us. And if you want to use you success to impact others, on our last day we will learn how to reach for the sky by changing our perspective and becoming a creator of change."

As the group started wrapping up for the day, Nancy gave each of them a backpack containing the materials they would need. As they all started talking about how ready they were to finally take this journey, the excitement in the room became palpable.

Suddenly, Gina said, "By the way, did everyone get the same invitation? It was so unusual—just a single question."

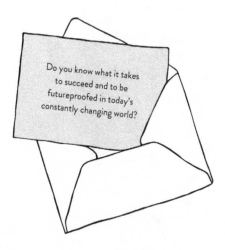

Do you know what it takes to succeed and to be futureproofed in today's constantly changing world?

THE NEW BLUEPRINT FOR SUCCESS AND *FUTUREPROOFING*

THE FIRST DAY STARTED with a group breakfast and a sightseeing tour of the truly majestic grounds of the nature retreat. The travelers enjoyed seeing the more than fifty land animals, 150 species of birds, and hundreds of plants all around them. The heart-stopping views and constant rush of water from the falls created an experience for all the senses. After a while, though, they turned their focus to the amazing red-rock formations and mountains in the distance. They decided they wanted to see these beautiful mountains up close, but they were not sure which of the many paths ahead would lead them there.

The Road to Success Is on Permanent Detour

NANCY LET THEM KNOW that the old road to the mountains was the path right in front of them. As she pointed to the path, they all saw the detour sign.

As they walked the old path, Nancy explained it was the path everyone was used to traveling. This road, with its three circles, was supposed to guide them all to the mountains, because even if they didn't realize it, they were already using a blueprint for how to get to success in life.

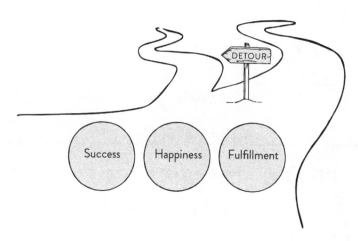

We're all familiar with the old path to success. We were told if we worked hard and climbed our company ladder, we would eventually achieve career and material success—better titles, more power, and the accompanying financial rewards. Nancy pointed out that such success was the first circle the travelers could see.

That success was supposed to lead to happiness, the second circle, and happiness was in turn supposed to lead to a sense of fulfillment in life. "That's the third circle you see," explained Nancy.

"As we used to define it," Nancy summarized, "success was largely seen through the lens of your career and how you were rewarded, and on your salary, promotions, and recognition. That in turn was supposed to lead to happiness, which in turn was supposed to lead to a sense of fulfillment."

As the travelers walked this old path, they realized after several hours of increasing fatigue and frustration that they were not getting any closer to the mountains. They were simply walking in circles.

Nancy pointed out that was because:

Career success does not automatically turn into the life success, happiness, and fulfillment we assumed would follow.

WHY DOESN'T THIS ROAD LEAD ANYWHERE?

GINA ASKED WHY THE road was on permanent detour. That's when the group saw written on another sign ahead:

> *Often people attempt to live their lives backward. They try to have more things or more money in order to do more of what they want so that they will be happier. The way it actually works is the reverse. You must first be who you really are and then do what you need to do in order to have what you want.*
>
> *—Margaret Young*

Nancy explained that the problem with the old road was that we usually started off seeing our life through the college major we picked and the path our first job started us on. In other words, we ended up defining everything we were—our *full selves*—by our college major and our first job. We then hoped this would magically lead to life fulfilment. In other words, the choices we made when we were teenagers ended up defining our value well into our fifties.

I'll Be Happy When . . .

ANOTHER REASON WE FAIL to achieve success is because of the "I'll be happy when" syndrome. On this path, we're supposed to keep checking things off the to-do list in order to get to happy. What ends up happening though, is we collect accomplishments and focus on the future to the detriment of living today because we're always trying to get to the next thing as quickly as possible.

This delaying of happiness can go on forever if we let it, because we've been told that the narrowly defined but powerful symbols of success we are chasing hold the key to happiness and fulfillment. But in the midst of all this busyness, and with no time left for ourselves, we start deferring not only our happiness but also our dreams. We instead start to make grand bargains: I will be happy when I get the next job, when I get the next promotion, when I have my first baby, when I move into my dream house. We start living in the future because we know that our *now* is not what we thought it would be. By then we've completely lost sight, or we never even looked, for what we really wanted. At some point we start to notice we are on a treadmill—with lots of motion that really isn't leading anywhere, just like the path to the mountains the group was on.

By the time we realize the path we are on isn't leading where we want to go, we've worked and sacrificed our most precious commodity—time with our families and time to do what we really want. And we've done it all in the name of being on the path to success. In the end, though, it seems we gave up too much with very little payoff.

It's a New World

ANOTHER PROBLEM WITH THE traditional path is that even if it *did* once lead us where we wanted to go, it is not built for the times we live in today. The world has changed—and we can no longer assume that having one successful career is the cornerstone of a lifetime of safety and security. That kind of success by itself no longer brings the assurance that we will always be able to provide for our needs and for those of our family, because this road no longer accounts for the twists and turns we must now prepare ourselves for. No matter how successful we may be today, we still feel vulnerable to what is around the corner.

Today, we need to be *FutureProofed*. We need to know how to *stay* on the journey we want, regardless of what life brings us in this fast-changing world. What's missing from this old path is the peace of mind that comes from knowing we can stay on course and thrive, regardless of what changes and disruptions come our way.

WHY MASLOW HAD IT WRONG

ANOTHER REASON THE OLD path no longer works has to do with Abraham Maslow[1] and his classic hierarchy of needs.

Maslow's Hierarchy

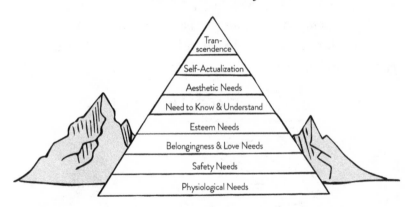

Maslow believed people are motivated to first fulfill basic needs, such as food, safety, love, and belonging, before they can move on to fulfilling more advanced needs. While every human being strives to fulfill higher needs like their fulfilling their potential and finding meaning and purpose, Maslow maintained that we first are driven to satisfy our more basic needs at the bottom of the pyramid *before* we satisfy the ones toward the top.

But Maslow had it wrong.

Along with a sense of safety and security, many people also want a sense of fulfillment, purpose, and meaning. They're not seeking fulfillment and meaning only after their basic needs are met. Most people want to do work that matters right now, not just after they have achieved a certain amount of financial security.

This conflict is at the root of the pain so many of us feel right now. It's a push-pull dilemma—the push toward personal fulfillment and meaning, the pull toward the security of a steady paycheck to provide for our needs. The group all agreed that they wanted to pursue their dreams but felt stuck in unfulfilling jobs so they could pay the bills. The simultaneous push-pull is what has led them to feeling trapped and yearning for something more.

At this point on their journey, the travelers realized they had now found another detour from the old path they were on. They decided to take that road instead.

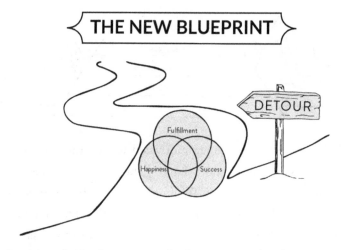

Looking down the new road, the group realized it was different from the one they were used to. Nancy suggested they think about where they wanted to go as being at the center of this road—and not at the *end*, like it was on the old road.

When we stand at the center of the new road, what we really want is:

- The sense of achievement and success that comes with doing work that matters to us.
- The peace of mind that comes from knowing we can be *Future-Proofed* regardless of what is around the next corner.
- To experience happiness and joy on a regular basis.
- The sense of fulfillment that comes from knowing we are living meaningfully.

It's the same for us as it was for Nancy's travelers. This is how we have redefined our new destination of success and *FutureProofing*, and this is what we now seek.

But this new path, unlike the last road, is no longer sequential. This means that what we really want to do is blur the boundaries between how we work, live, and play. We want to merge both our personal and professional worlds such that our daily lives are a manifestation of who we truly are. We want to be fully engaged and present in our lives.

The road we want to travel is one where we get up each day caring deeply about our work. We want to be engaged in relationships, activities, and interests that bring joy to our lives, regardless of how busy and harried our lives may be. And we want the peace of mind that comes from knowing we are *FutureProofed* because we're equipped with the skills we need to navigate this new path even in a constantly changing world.

Ultimately, as Nancy told her travelers, we *all* know there is something deeper and more valuable inside us than the previous path led us to believe. But we often get lost on the old path, just like Nancy's travelers did on that original road. We get lost in the day-to-day struggle to keep ourselves afloat in choppy waters. We get lost in the busyness of our lives. We get lost in achieving and accomplishing. And we get lost in reaching for momentary happiness.

The travelers agreed, but added that even though the old path no longer led anywhere, at least they knew what to do—it was a step-by-step walk. And even though they now knew they were supposed to travel to a sweet spot, they were not exactly sure how to travel this new path.

Nancy said the real challenge for us all now is, how do we take this new journey we really want to take? How do we get to this new destination—this new sweet spot?

She let them know that throughout this journey, they were going to learn to do exactly what the sign they just saw told them they needed to do: they were going to *first* learn to be who they really are and *then* learn to do what they now need to do in order to have what they now really want to have.

Your Compass and Your Clocks

NANCY TOLD THEM THAT the first step on this new journey was learning how to view themselves outside of the narrow lens of their college major and job titles. To do so, instead of traveling this new path step by step as we've all been taught, they were going to think of the three circles as bringing together their compass and their clocks.

As Dr. Stephen Covey described[2], think of your compass as being your bigger vision for your life. It represents what you deeply care about, what you feel is important, and what gives meaning to your existence. Consider this as being how you want to lead your life based on who you really are.

Your clocks, on the other hand, are how you end up spending your time on a day-to-day basis. On this journey we are taking, there are two clocks; one clock is how you use your talents and skills for work, and the other clock is how you spend your time at play—the things you do for fun and that bring joy.

On the old path, we thought that time-telling—in other words, seeing ourselves mainly through our work clock, was supposed to lead to happiness, which in turn was supposed to lead to finding our larger life vision or compass, and with it, a sense of meaning and fulfillment.

Now we see clearly why, even under the best of circumstances, the old path was largely a road to nowhere because our life journey just doesn't work that way.

We all knew this step-by-step time-telling was not working for us, even if we did not have a good way to explain it. The pain the travelers all talked about when they arrived is what we all feel when our compass and clocks are working against each other or when they're not functioning at all.

For instance, as Bobby described on his first day, there is a deep yearning when we live without that bigger vision to our life but we know enough to time-tell and get by in the here and now.

When we live without joy, it feels as if we are just existing. There are no highs as we go through the motions each day to just get through, just as Roberta talked about.

We feel a deep sense of anxiety, as Mark described, when we don't feel we can use our skills and talents to provide for ourselves and control what happens in our life.

Shelly described how money alone does not provide all that we want because it guarantees neither happiness nor fulfillment.

And as Gina described, knowing what is meaningful to us in the long run without knowing what to do in the here and now to get there just leaves us with the yearning to do what matters to us without knowing how to pay the bills today.

Even without being able to name it exactly, we usually know that something is off. Sometimes the feeling is vague; we know we're confused and that something is just not right. Other times it's too painful to ignore and feels like we're in crisis.

At other times, our clocks will remind us through some big life marker that there is a disconnect between our compass and our clocks. For example, sometimes our birthday can cause us to reflect on our life and ask ourselves if we are where we thought we would be at that point. We often find that all the time-telling we've done along the way did not get us any closer to our compass goals and dreams.

But when our compass and our clocks are aligned, we are able to close the gap between where we are and what we hope to accomplish in our lives as well as experience the peace of mind, joy, and fulfillment we seek.

A New View of Success

AT THIS POINT IN the journey, Nancy's travelers notice that the mountains which were previously in the distance, are now in close view.

While they look at the beautiful mountains, Nancy tells them that we normally approach our lives by taking a bottom-up approach—the same way we would climb a mountain. We just start climbing and traveling up, starting with our college major and first job, often with no good idea of how to reach the mountain peak.

Here's the problem: the more we live, the more we end up burying and filtering our real compass, our own way to our own mountain peak. So it's not a surprise that so many of us become really good time-tellers: we do and achieve and accomplish, but we're off course. We then realize there is almost no connection between our compass and our clocks, and it becomes even more painful when we realize we are not *FutureProofed*. The skills and strategies we learned that brought us to this place no longer seem to take us where we really want to go because of the constant waves of change coming at us.

The good news is that we are going to learn an entirely new way to travel, by taking a top-down view on our life instead of the bottom up view we are used to. We are going to take a very different perspective on our life so we can see who we really are by learning what we must know about our own compass and clocks.

Nancy and the travelers then went to the airport and got on a plane. As they flew over the mountains, Nancy said, "If I asked you right now if you knew the bigger vision for your life—what will bring you a sense of fulfillment, meaning, and purpose—would you know that clearly?"

They looked at each other in silence.

"You probably don't have a good idea of how to answer this question because most of us have never identified our bigger vision," Nancy explained. "Maybe we did, but we've covered over our big picture with all our time-telling. So first, we need to *unfilter* our lives and discover or rediscover what matters most to us."

Shelly asked, "Why is it that as we get older, our vision for ourselves seems to get buried under or filtered through lots of other things?"

"It's because as children, we are all born with unique gifts and talents," Nancy said. "We knew what we liked to do even if we didn't have all the words to explain it. This is part of how we built our confidence as kids. But as we got older and continued to interact with others—whether they were family members, peers, or just the world around us—this natural sense of who we were started to fade into the background. What took center stage instead was all the things we were supposed to be and do to conform to what was expected of us and to the external standards around us."

Nancy went on to explain another challenge we all face. When we set out to build successful careers by developing skills that allow us to provide for ourselves and our families, those skills are not always the ones we care most deeply about. But because we usually interpret our lives through the narrow lens of the skills we have built up (time-telling), it later becomes difficult for us to see ourselves without the filter of what we have thus far been rewarded for.

Whether it's for financial security or for social rewards and acceptance, we often lose sight of what is most true about us. We stop connecting—or even trying to connect—with our compass because of our daily obligations of time-telling. But without a connection to our compass, we don't even know when we are trading away things that really mean something to us, because we haven't put the right value on those things in the first place. If we never even try to find our compass, we end up feeling like we are drifting in the wind—chasing a bunch of goals that shift and change—because there's no big picture for our life. If we at some point *did* connect with our inner compass but we buried it for some reason, we live with constant pain and yearning for what we lost.

The Wrong Way to Find Your Compass

> *When you do what you always did, you'll get what you always got.*
>
> —*Albert Einstein*

WHEN WE ARE TRYING to find a clearer direction in life we are often told to write purpose statements. While that *sounds* good, it can be an exercise in frustration. When we don't know our bigger vision or how to figure it out, we just end up putting words on paper that are lost and forgotten as quickly as they are written.

Most of us have either not discovered or have deeply buried who we really are. By immediately trying to write a purpose statement, we treat the *symptom*, not the problem itself, because we are creating a big purpose statement while standing inside of our filtered view of our life.

We have no idea how to view our lives without all the filters, much less how to figure out our bigger vision and purpose. Beautifully crafted statements may sound good, but ultimately—like the road that loops in circles—they go nowhere.

Instead of writing a life-purpose statement from our filtered perspective, then, we should first address the root cause of the problem—the disconnection from ourselves.

How to Find Your Compass and Clocks

LET'S TAKE A DIFFERENT perspective on this important *where-to* question so we can see ourselves differently. When we think about where we are going, it is usually through the lens of our skills and competencies *in our careers*. We need to first free ourselves of this narrow perspective because it will lead us to a vision that's too limited.

That is why we are flying thirty-thousand feet in the air. From this vantage point, we can stand outside of our life and look *from above* it rather than standing inside it. The higher we fly, the thinner the air becomes and the less drag we experience. There is also less turbulence at higher altitudes. All of this allows us to have a clearer view of our compass.

During this plane ride, we will fly at different altitudes and see the big picture of our life with increasing clarity, rather than looking from the bottom-up as we normally do. As we fly, we will learn the four steps we need to know to unfilter our lives. That way, no matter what twists and turns our life takes, we always know how to chart our own course and stay on our path. These four steps will also prepare us to learn the new blueprint for success and *FutureProofing* during the rest of our journey together.

29

Step One: You Unfiltered

Moments That Matter

HERE'S HOW IT WORKS: Choose a place to go. It should be a place—past, present, or future—that means something to you. We are looking for the *Moments That Matter* in your life. A moment or moments that when you think of your life, it lifts above all moments.

You should go to a moment that you think will help bring you into sharper focus, and not just look at yourself through the greys that come when we filter our life.

Here are a few ideas to get you started in finding your *moments that matter:*

- Go on a dig and describe what you find.
- Look into the future and decide what you want to be remembered for. What will others say about you when you're gone?
- When was the last sighting of you?
- What is challenging, exciting, fulfilling, engaging?
- Is there a moment in time that means something to you?
- Is there a place that matters to you?

These ideas should start to *awaken* your senses so that you start to see yourself unfiltered. You might awaken your senses with a moment that provokes you, inspires you, something you aspire to, something that engages you deeply, something that makes you uncomfortable, something you remember, something you want, or anything else you think of that matters to you because it *stirs* something in you.

Five Visits

YOU MAY ALSO BE inspired by the moments Nancy's five travelers described:

"I want to take you to the future so I can hear what will be said about me at my funeral," Gina said. "What I want said is that I was able to truly live and that I helped make this world a better place. I want to know I left this world better than I found it. Right now, I have lots of social media friends—many likes and followers. But what I really want is for people to say I used my love of writing in a way that allowed me to contribute to helping others and our planet. If that was said about me, I would know my time here on earth meant something."

"I decided to make myself uncomfortable by taking away the gift of time," Bobby explained. "I want to think about what my life would be like if I found out I only had a year to live. I want to think about what I would do if I had nothing to lose, because it would force me to think about my life differently. With nothing to lose, I would think about risks differently. I'm really much more creative than I get to be right now, but I always end up staying quiet and talking myself out of so much. When I see my ideas come to life later, I always wish I had followed my instincts instead of the crowd. I'm letting myself down right now, so I want to stay uncomfortable until I figure out where I belong and what I want to do."

Going next, Roberta said, "I want to visit the place I last saw myself—my college campus. That was the last time I felt full of hope and promise. It was a time when so much was happening in the world around us, and I just knew, I *really believed*, that I too was going to leave my mark on the world. I used to tutor kids when I was in college because that mattered to me. When I graduated, I had to become safe, pay the bills, and take care of the kids. I left that girl full of promise behind. Everyone else's dreams became my dreams, and I lost sight of my own."

Mark also wanted to visit the past, traveling "back to the time when my twins were born." The home we were in at that time was the house we lost when I lost my job. It was the place that felt like home. I am going back to the day we brought the twins home from the hospital. All I needed was my family. I had just gotten a promotion at work, but what I remember is that while I was happy about the promotion, the job itself wasn't what mattered most. The control over my life that I felt was what was priceless. I remember looking in my daughters' eyes and how that made me feel. I saw the future in their eyes, and I felt loved.

Shelly wanted to go on a dig. "That's because I know if I dig deep enough, I will find the real me. I would find a jump rope, because the jump rope reminds me of when I was on the playground as a kid. It reminds me of when it was okay to be dirty, to fall off the swings, to fail, to be my own boss, and to be anything else I chose. That was one of the few times growing up that I didn't need to chase praise. I didn't need to value what other people thought like it was my oxygen. I didn't need to be perfect; I just needed to be me. The second thing I would find is the business plan I put together a couple years ago. It represents me taking full charge of my life, but I always find a way to bury that, too."

Step Two: Your Compass

What Is Meaningful Action?

ONCE WE HAVE AWAKENED our senses at the thirty-thousand-foot level, the next step is to fly at a lower altitude. This means we will go from finding *moments that matter* at thirty-thousand feet above ground to observing the patterns of our lives from ten-thousand feet in the air. Uncovering those patterns will give us more clues to our compass and clocks.

Nancy told them that they are going to try to get closer to what is meaningful to them, so she asked them to consider:

- What do you care about deeply?
- What matters to you?
- What holds value for you?
- What gets you really excited?
- When you think about yourself at your best, what does that mean to you?
- What inspires you to do what you do?
- What do you believe in deeply?
- Is there anything you learned from your flight at thirty-thousand-feet that may be useful now?

She asked them to spend some time at this altitude, and to put some thoughts on sticky notes for themselves.

Bobby noted that Nancy did not ask the question most people ask which is, "What is your life purpose?" Nancy said that is because for some people, they know early in their life what is their purpose. For others, it evolves over time and experiences in their life. It sometimes becomes clearer after seeing our own pattern of what we keep coming back to, and what continues to matter to us above all else, but this requires experience and paying attention to our patterns. In the meantime, we all can connect to something we care deeply about. If that happens to be your purpose, then great, if not, it does not matter, just start where you are. This is a journey, and as beginners, we are all a work in progress.

As you think about what you deeply care about from this perspective, try to brainstorm without any filters. No wordsmithing. You don't need to share your thoughts with anyone—so don't worry about making what you care about sound big, lofty, or important in the eyes of others. Just be true to yourself about what matters most to you.

_____

_____

_____

_____

Step Three: Your Clocks

What Is Effortless Action?

NOW IT'S TIME TO drop down to the five-thousand-foot level so we can uncover what is effortless action in our life—in other words, we are going to look more closely at our work and play clocks.

What we're trying to discover, both in our areas of work and play, is what feels effortless to us. When are we in a state of flow?

What Is Flow?

Flow, according to Mihaly Csikszentmihalyi is a state in which people are so involved in an activity that nothing else seems to matter.[3]

When you are in a state of flow and using your gifts and talents, you are going to be very motivated to do that thing. When you are in flow, doing the activity is rewarding in and of itself. You may have heard it referred to as being "in the zone." It's a state that leads to a sense of joy regardless of what the activity is. In these moments of flow, your being is highly aligned with your doing, you're unaware of the passing of time, and you don't worry about failure because challenges you are facing perfectly mesh with your abilities to meet them.

Now let's spend some time writing down key times in our life when we felt our actions were effortless and we were in a state of flow, whether for work or play.

Here's a tip as you think about and write down a few of these key times of being in the zone. Notice that I did not ask you separate questions for your work and play clocks. It is because in my many years of experience, whether as a professional or personal leadership consultant, I have found that looking at when we are in the zone, regardless of whether we are at work or play, is the best way to help unfilter our lives. When we open our lives up to stories beyond what happens in our adult work life and also look at times when we were younger, we tend to get the most unfiltered view and some of the most powerful experiences in our life. So, don't worry about categories or labels, just think about the stories of when you are in the zone.

_____

_____

_____

_____

Step Four: Your Why

The Power of Patterns

FOR THEIR FINAL EXPERIENCE of the day, Nancy said, "Now, let me ask you a question you likely have not thought about as you looked at all you wrote for what is meaningful and effortless to you. Do you see any patterns so far? Are there any patterns that help you understand what makes your meaningful and effortless actions so magnetic to you? In other words, your _why_?

"Here is what I mean by this question. There is always a reason for _why_ we do what we do. It is usually for something we ultimately want, for something _we'll get in return,_ that is a constant pull in our life no matter what we do. Knowing _why_ we are drawn to what we choose is what helps to give our compass, our true north, its magnetic quality.

"So, for example, for some, when they look at all the things that matter to them, and when they think of the common denominator of _why_ they do what they do, they see that what they get from all those experiences are things like:

Self-Oriented

- _Being their Best_—Some ultimately want full self-expression. They are at their highest when they can use their talents and gifts to perform at their best.

- *Being the Best*—Some focus on excelling against others. They revel in the ability to be number one when compared to others.

Challenge-Oriented

- *Reaching a Goal*—These people need a goal to strive for. They thrive on having something that allows them to measure their performance and define whether they have achieved the goal.

- *Problem Solving*—These people are at their highest and finest when there is a tough problem to solve. They love the opportunity to dig in and find solutions in ways others cannot.

Improvement-Oriented

- *Making It Better*—These people love to create or innovate—whether products, services, or anything else. They love taking something or spotting a need and finding a way to make it better.

- *Empowering People*—For these people, it is not about the goal itself but about helping other people grow and perform at their best. They are at their finest when working with others.

- *Influencing Others*—For these people, it is about the influence they can have on changing other people's behaviors through their opinions, leadership, and overall influence.

Learning-Oriented

- *Learning*—For some, it's not about the destination, it's about the learning process involved and the knowledge they gain.

World-Oriented

- *Accomplishing a Mission*—These people want to be a part of something bigger than themselves. They want to see the difference they can make in the lives of others and want the world to be a better place for all.

To get to your *why*, spend a few moments looking for any patterns in what you care deeply about and stories of when you are in the zone.

As you look for patterns, watch out for this trap: Sometimes we confuse the *what*, *where*, and *why*. Here's a perfect example: someone who works in a cause-based nonprofit may have an ultimate *why* of full self-expression—they want to be at their best. Working at the nonprofit is simply the place where they express their *why*. For them, their *why* it is not really about the cause or the mission, it is really about being able to perform at their best. Conversely, many people in the private sector use their work as a way to connect them to a larger mission, something they truly care about beyond themselves. They are deeply passionate about their work because of the impact they want to have beyond themselves through their product or service. Many people are both world oriented *and* oriented in other ways, such as being challenge oriented. The important question to ask yourself is, regardless of *what* you do and *where* you do it, *why* do you do it?

As you look at what you brainstormed, do you see any pattern or patterns that reveal *why* you do what you do?

You Unfiltered

As THEY BEGIN TO head back to the airport, Nancy told them the key point they should take from all that they did on their journey today was that they needed to fly above their life so they could start to look from a different perspective and *unfilter* it so they could begin to see who they are outside of the narrow lens of job titles. They could do so by seeing the patterns that emerged in their lives regarding *why* they kept doing what they did, even without realizing it.

What is most natural to you? What are the things that mean something to you? Why do those things mean something to you, and what do you just naturally want to do that brings you to being one with yourself? Knowing these things is what is already guiding your life—it is your true north and helps to give your life a sense of direction even without you knowing it.

Uncovering and developing your compass and your clocks is not a one-and-done exercise. It is about allowing the patterns that emerge and what comes naturally to you to come forth. The more you live and do, the more clues you will discover along the way, until things start to come into sharper focus.

Once the travelers landed, Nancy told them there was a large canvas hanging on the wall in their cabins and plenty of sticky notes so that they could keep working on what they'd started. They were to continue throughout the journey defining the moments that mattered and why they mattered, what was meaningful action and why, and the things, whether for work or play that were effortless and naturally pulled at them.

You should do the same. Keep adding to your canvas so you can see patterns over time in the things you experience. The more you create a habit of looking for the patterns in your life and the *why*, the clearer your life will become.

THE NEW CAREER PLAYBOOK

THE NEXT MORNING, THE travelers were chatting over breakfast and reflecting on their first day. Shelly talked about what an aha moment it was for her to see *why* the old step-by-step path didn't lead anywhere. Roberta and Gina talked about how freeing it was to just be okay with the fact that their life compass and clocks were not yet clear and that this journey would help them figure it out. Bobby loved the way it helped him think about his *why*, and Mark said that realizing the difference between his compass and clocks was a real eye-opener for him.

Nancy joined the group and began the day by letting them know that while yesterday was about how to begin our journey by being who we truly are, today's journey was about learning what we all now *must do differently* to get what we want and to live inside the sweet spot that was coming into sharper focus. She also explained that today they were going to focus on their work clock and the new world of work.

We are starting here first because so much of the vulnerability and anxiety we feel comes from the fact that the world of work has changed and we don't know how to adjust our journey in response. And it's not just figuring out how to navigate differently—it's also about how to be *FutureProofed* to make sure we know how to keep ourselves moving toward and living in our life sweet spot, regardless of any changes that occur.

The Old Paradigm: The Fallacy of One

FOR THE FIRST STOP of the day, the travelers found themselves in a boat docked in a small harbor. It was a perfect place to talk about the "fallacy of one." One major. One career. One plan. One path. Doing it all alone.

"Before now," Nancy explained, "that's how we were told to travel. We were also told that our education and hard work would lead to success and security throughout our lives. There were fewer choices on the old path, and we learned early on how to navigate inside those narrow lanes. There was a lane for someone who wanted to be in the medical profession for example, as a doctor or a nurse. There was a lane for people who wanted to be in finance or business or teaching, and so on. In those narrow lanes, land was always in sight, and lots of signposts marked the way. In many ways, then, that was considered the *safe harbor.*"

The Insecurity of Job Security: Rethinking Risk and the True Grand Bargain

WE USED TO THINK that once we found our lane and a good job in that lane, the job it would last us a lifetime and we would have a sense of security. We would never have to worry again. As long as we paid our dues and gave our skills and talents to our company, we would be rewarded in exchange with the trappings of success, like promotions and prestige in the short run, and job stability, and security in the long run.

Regardless of how true or not that grand bargain turned out to be in the past, there's another big problem with it today. That employment contract no longer exists. In its place is a short-term agreement. The payoff we expected for our loyalty no longer exists. The recession and its aftermath taught us that there's no such thing as job security. According to Bureau of Labor statistics,[1] the median number of years an employee now stays at their job is 4.2 years. Companies no longer invest in things like career development the way they used to in part because we are no longer expected to commit years of our life working just for them.

But even with this broken contract, there was another problem with this grand bargain we made with employers: the fine print said that success would come by working hard and *waiting* for someone else, usually your boss, to notice you and help you move your career forward. But you needed to wait for someone else to tell you which of your skills were most valuable, wait for the next promotion, and wait to get someone else's permission to explore other avenues if that was what you wanted to do.

In this grand bargain, then, your value was based on *what someone else decided.*

Think about that for a minute.

One person held the ability to move you forward—or hold you back. Your boss, not you, ultimately controlled your career. The irony was that the higher we climbed up the company ladder, the more at risk we felt, because it was now no longer just our job on the line; it was our family health insurance, our home mortgage, our car payments, the kids' college tuition, and so on. In exchange for this thing called "security," we handed the keys to our life to someone else.

In other words, the "safe harbor" wasn't so safe after all.

What is clear is that:

The world of work has dramatically changed, but what we are told about how to navigate it has not really changed at all.

The World of Work Has Changed

THE NEXT STOP FOR the travelers, Nancy said, was to move from the harbor to the open seas. That's because in a more networked, globalized, and competitive world and with a different expectation than just one job for life, that's exactly what the path feels like—open seas.

That's both good and bad news. The good news is that there are now many paths to follow and many ways to follow those paths. This means there are many more ways to move toward your sweet spot than the small number of old career ladders. The bad news is that you can become overwhelmed and lose yourself in the process. The pathways often feel disconnected, and it is not at all clear how to navigate some of these paths. Rather than appreciating the vastness of the options, you can instead feel like you're drifting at the mercy of the open seas.

Let's talk about risk again. In the safe harbor, we saw a downside to the old path. But now, even though the world of work has dramatically changed, we don't really tell people what the new rules are so that they can navigate the open seas. Instead, we often just encourage them to go do stuff, try lots of things, and follow their passion. While that advice is not completely wrong, the advice is incomplete. No one should just jump into the open sea headfirst without a strategy for what to do and how to navigate this new context.

The truth is, there is often good reason why people are hesitant to jump headfirst. Lots of people are afraid that if they take a risk and just jump in without really understanding the open seas, they may put not only themselves at risk but also the people who depend on them. Many of us were severely impacted by the recession; some of us are still recovering. Many still feel that sense of vulnerability so they are trying not to make blind decisions that could put them at further risk.

Today, many people are just a few paychecks away from not being able to recover from some unseen disaster, and know they are walking a financial tightrope. The real question for us all now, is how to navigate these waters and thrive without feeling even more vulnerable.

What people really want and need is a way to think about and manage this changing context that not only steadies them on choppy waters but helps them get from where they are to where they really want to be.

The New Playbook for Success and FutureProofing

As the travelers return to land from the open seas, they arrive at an open area with an obstacle course that has modified rock-climbing walls. They first see walls that are steep but doable. After looking around for a minute, they see other climbing walls that look more like ramps that aren't as hard to climb.

These modified climbing walls represent the journey we must now learn to take in the new world of work. There are lots of features on these climbing walls. Some of them look like ladders, some look like rocks, and some feature footholds where it would be easy to climb. Some look like little bridges that connect one place to another. The walls shift from time to time, and sometimes the footholds don't appear until someone tries to take a step. By looking at the walls, it's obvious to the travelers that there are many more ways to get to the top, but they don't know how to take advantage of it all and how to decide on the best way to navigate.

Nancy tells her travelers that their challenge is to learn the seven moves they need to make and how to use ropes, harnesses, and protective gear to make their climbing wall go from the steeper wall it looks like now, to the much more manageable ramps that they also see.

As Nancy puts each traveler in front of a climbing wall, each tries to climb his or her wall without any instruction. They all start off feeling very unsteady. That unsteadiness is because right now what is seared into our brain, and what we're all familiar with, is that academic success equals life success. So, all we needed were the academic skills we learned in the classroom and the diploma we earned as the ticket for being able to climb our career ladder.

That's no longer true. In today's environment, here's what you need to know and what you need to do to climb successfully.

Next Level

SINCE THE WORLD OF work has changed, we can no longer simply think about getting our next job. Instead, we need to think about having more choices and more control over our lives. This change in perspective requires a whole new strategy and playbook, so that no matter what happens—no matter which way the wind blows or how the ground is shifting under us—we can always move toward our sweet spot.

As we have seen though, having too many choices but no strategy for how to manage those choices can shut us down and overwhelm us. We need a way of organizing all our options and a way of creating a new playbook with plays that work to our advantage as well as ways of creating new plays and more choices so we can make our journey successfully and securely.

In order to go from learning how to find our next job, to learning how to create a lifelong career playbook, the first thing we need to know is that we will approach this climb differently than we have approached our work before.

You Must Be the Boss of Your Own Life

THE NUMBER ONE CAREER mistake that most of us make is that we spend so much time researching and learning about the next business we might want to work for, but almost no time learning about the business of *You*. What I mean is you must see yourself as the boss of your own life and be willing to take full control of your career, regardless of what business you're in or whether you work for someone else or for yourself. Instead of thinking of yourself as being in the job market only when you are unhappy or laid off, you must always be open to as many new opportunities as you can be. By creating a playbook of all of the ways you can make a living using your skills and talents, you always have more choices and you can position yourself for success on *your* terms.

This also means that you must have a no-permission-required attitude and mindset. You no longer need to wait for anyone to appoint you, anoint you, or otherwise deem you worthy of stepping up and into new opportunities. You do not need to wait for others to notice your talent. You must be the one to determine your own value and the impact you want to make.

Step One: Create Your Own Markers for Success

NANCY TELLS THE GROUP that it's time to get started. As they all look at their walls and prepare for their climb, they notice that it's hard to climb because there are no markers to help them figure out a path upward. She tells them that the first thing they are going to do, is create their own markers for success.

When you heard "markers for success," you probably thought that meant your job or career markers. We've already talked about the wrong way to find our compass. Now let's talk about what else we do wrong that practically assures we'll never get where we want to be.

We usually create purpose statements and vision boards over a weekend when we have the time and space to breathe. But by Monday morning, when we are once again swept up in our lives, we go right back to the busyness of our schedules, and we start the time-telling all over again. Please don't misunderstand my point: purpose statements and vision boards and other tools like them are very helpful if done right and used well. Why, then, do they end up being practically useless? It is because we create big-picture statements and boards but track only the markers of success for our next job or for moving up in our career. We never *track our bigger life compass markers*. In other words, we don't know how to track if we are being successful in the long run. We only end up tracking what is happening in this moment, so we never really figure out how to track anything more than what our employers are asking of us—time-telling.

Only when life's big milestones (like birthdays) come up do we reflect, and only then do we realize we are not making the progress on our bigger life vision we had hoped for. Instead, what we need to do *first* is figure out what the markers for our big vision are that will tell us if we are on the right track. Those markers must be both what we want to do and how we want to feel, because we are both human beings and human doings.

Take a moment and look at the list of the things you care deeply about, which you started earlier. Look, too, at your thoughts on why those things are so magnetic to you—your *why*. Jot down a concise statement of what you care deeply about at this point. Don't stress about making it perfect or final; just get something down in writing to get you started.

_____

_____

_____

_____

Now, create a few compass success markers for yourself. To do that, decide how you will know you are moving toward your big vision. What must you do, and how must you feel?

_____

_____

_____

_____

Step Two: Create Your Playbook and Manage Risk

The biggest risk of all is not taking one.
                                                    —*Mellody Hobson*

NOW THAT YOU'VE CREATED your success markers, you need to create your playbook so the vastness of the wall you're about to climb doesn't feel so intimidating.

Let's return to what we usually do wrong to ensure we never get where we are wanting to go. What we currently do is take our purpose statements, and not only do we *not* create success markers for our larger vision, but we walk a path that was crafted *only* through the lens of one job title. The problem with this strategy is that your job title leaves you with only one way forward.

By now, we all know we need to diversify our retirement portfolios to hedge against risk. In the same way, we should have more than one play and more than one way to make our journey. We need to not just develop one plan in one lane but instead learn how to create a playbook with many lanes and opportunities—all of which we continue to update as our needs change.

Gone are the days when having a larger salary spelled security. In fact, building a larger lifestyle from one employer's paycheck is the *opposite* of security. You're not *FutureProofed*; you're building a very tall house of cards that could topple the minute a strong wind blows into your life. It's an outdated scenario that gives one person too much control over your future (especially since that one person isn't *you*).

Now as we make our journey, we need to be able to reach into our backpack and pull out not just a diploma and a job title but a variety of ways to make a play, regardless of whether we are working for someone else or for ourselves. We need to shift how we see ourselves to include ways that open up many more choices right from the start.

The Story We Tell Ourselves

THE STORY WE TELL ourselves about ourselves is the most important story there is. The reason your story is so important is because it helps you make sense of your life and your experiences. It helps you define who you are; it shapes how you think, what you believe, the choices you make, and the actions you take. If the story you tell yourself is too narrow, it will limit your ability to grow and evolve. If your identity is based on a job title and that title disappears, your narrow story of yourself will limit what you believe you can do next.

I Am Not My Job Title

WHEN MILLIONS OF PEOPLE lost their jobs in the recession, there was a lot of attention paid to not just the financial devastation the job losses caused but also to what it meant for people, often men, and their sense of who they were. As a frequent radio guest as a business expert and psychologist on the subject, what callers consistently said was that they grew up being taught to see themselves and to define their value based on their roles in their jobs. So while it was true that after the recession they were struggling to figure out how they were going to pick up the pieces and reinvent their career in the wake of the job loss, the pain and vulnerability of not having any idea who they were *separate* from their titles and roles that were now gone was the most palpable pain. In the past, they were able to use their titles as the stand-in to represent who they were. The problem was, when that was gone, so was their identity.

Even if the situation in your life isn't as dramatic as a job loss, and you are instead looking ahead and anticipating the future, we no longer expect to have one job for life and there are now many more ways to work. Given that we are now increasingly using our skills in many different ways, the more traditional job titles are often not enough to convey the full story of what we do.

The fact is that we usually start our journey to career success too small. We begin based on our first major and first job, and we lock ourselves into that story and identity. But doing so cuts off our ability to see anything not contained in that narrow story of ourselves.

A *Bigger* I Am

IF WE WANT TO open as many plays as possible for ourselves, we can't just see ourselves as nothing more than a job title. Instead, we need to see ourselves as the *why* behind what we do. That bigger why was what we were uncovering as we were unfiltering our compass, because that's what has the magnetic quality. The *why* is what we are after, not the job title. It's what we keep coming back to over and over, no matter what we do in life.

To change our story of ourself, we need to change our *I Am*. Let me share an example of what I mean by that. My first career was as a practicing clinical psychologist. But when I changed my awareness of myself from, *I Am a psychologist* to what is my why—what is magnetic for me: *I Am a problem solver who wants to have a positive impact in the world,* that switch opened up ways for me to be a problem solver in different industries and sectors with people, teams, executives, companies, organizations, and foundations.

That simple change allowed me to see many more ways in which I could make a play. Being a psychologist is simply one way for me to express my *why*. It is not the sum total. My playbook is made up of all the ways I can problem solve, not all the ways I can be a psychologist.

Gina gave another example: "Rather than seeing myself as a writer, what I am really after, my why, if I think about when I come alive as a writer, and my large social media platform, is *I want to have influence.* I want to use my talents to influence others and to help change how we think and what we do, for the greater good."

Now it is your turn. Continue to work on finding your *why,* which is a way to think of yourself that signals not a job title but what you ultimately see as what you get in return, regardless of your actual job title. Your *why* must mean something to you and must allow you to open more opportunities for yourself.

Building Your Playbook

Ideate

To *ideate* is to think outside the box in a way that stimulates free thinking and provides many ideas to choose from which to choose.

NOW THAT YOU HAVE a bigger *I Am*, you need a strategy to help you brainstorm, or ideate more potential plays for your playbook that you can make beyond the typical ones you already know. But before you start, here's a word about what this is and what this isn't. This ideating is not about coming up with a random list of all the things you can possibly do regardless of your interest, nor is it based on the typical stories of people who made lots of money in a short amount of time.

Remember, this is not just about finding your next job. Instead, this is about creating a lifelong strategy for how to take the vastness of the ocean and its constant change, and use it to your advantage so you can always recover from a setback, find new opportunities, or create new opportunities, all in a way that will lead you to where you want to go, not just to where someone else went.

Finding Your Predictable Patterns

TO BUILD YOUR PLAYBOOK, you are going to start with finding your predictable patterns. The last time you found your predictable pattern, it was your why. This time, finding your predictable patterns means thinking about your patterns of gifts, talents, strengths, the ways you like to work, how you relate to other people, and so on. By doing this, you will always be leading yourself to your sweet spot from a position of effortless power.

While there is no one question, tool, or assessment that will reveal everything you need, let's talk about some of the big categories of information—the kind of self-knowledge that is critical, as well as a few questions right now that you can ask yourself to help you get started.[2]

Talents and Strengths

A *talent* is a naturally recurring pattern of thought, feeling, or behavior that you use to do something unusually well.

A *strength* is the ability to consistently provide near perfect performance in a specific activity. Your strengths are a combination of your talents, knowledge, and building of skills.

Your Assets

IF YOU RECALL THE exercise you did earlier about thinking of times when you have been in flow, those stories offer a big clue to your talents and strengths. To help you further hone in on your talents and strengths, ask yourself questions like:

- Which projects have I spent hours on without getting tired?
- What things do I do easily and naturally that seem to be difficult for others?
- What tasks do I do that make me feel the most engaged and energized?

- What qualities are so signature to me that I cannot imagine myself without them?
- What do I do especially well?
- What seems easy to learn and do?
- What activities was I drawn to as a child?
- What activities completely immerse me?

Your Predictable Perspective

Now, AS YOU LOOK at your list of talents and strengths, to help you spot patterns in your assets, ask yourself this question:

When I am working on a team, what perspective do I naturally take?

- Do I tend to be the big-picture person, the idea person, the visionary? or
- Do I prefer to be the translator between big ideas and how others receive them, such as the communicator, or the influencer? or
- Do I tend to be more involved in the execution of projects such as developing others, organizing things, and implementing plans? or
- Do I tend to look beneath the surface by researching, investigating, or analyzing things?

Your Predictable Style

JOHN HOLLAND WAS A psychologist who developed one of the most well-known career assessments, Holland's Six Personality Types[3]. His big idea was that the jobs we choose are an expression of our personality. In other words, the choices we make in selecting a career are based on predictable patterns of how we like to channel oour work and the ways we like to relate to others while we work. He defined six tendencies, with the understanding that most people are a mix of a few.

Ask yourself which ones best describe your patterns of how you like to work:

- Do you like to work with animals, tools, or machines? Do you have athletic ability and prefer the outdoors? Do you tend to avoid activities like teaching?

- Do you like to study and solve math or science problems? Do you like to analyze, evaluate, and solve problems? Do you tend to avoid leading, selling, or persuading people?

- Do you have artistic or innovative abilities? Do you prefer to work in more unstructured situations where you can use your creativity? Do you avoid highly repetitive activities?

- Do you like to work with people? Do you like to counsel or give information? Do you tend to avoid using machines or tools to get things done?

- Do you like to lead and influence people and to sell things and ideas? Do you tend to avoid activities that require more scientific and analytical thinking?

- Do you like to work with numbers and data in a structured, detailed way? Do you tend to avoid ambiguous and unstructured activities?

Your Interests

In order to make sure that you end up brainstorming a list of possible playbook options that also represent your broader interests and activities that bring you joy, ask yourself:

- How else do you like to spend your time?
- What do you like to do for fun?

- What are the populations, groups, and customers with whom you like to work?
- What are some sectors and industries that may be interesting to you?

Broaden Your View

ONCE YOU HAVE FOUND your bigger *why* and identified your predictable patterns, you can broaden your sense of what you can do based on things you may not have even known about.

But before we broaden your view, let's talk about the difference between deliberately shifting between opportunities and just drifting from one thing to the next.

While we no longer have the same expectations for staying in our jobs for a lifetime, we should also avoid the other extreme of job hopping from one thing to the next with no larger purpose or way to connect our moves.

Career shifting is when you are taking your bigger vision, talents, strengths, skills, and predictable patterns, and using these as a basis for moving from one opportunity to the next, rather than using your job title. Shifting means that even when you are making a series of moves, there are some things that will remain consistent, or essentially true about you, as a way to help connect the moves so you do not just drift along aimlessly.

Let me give you an example of what I mean.

Earlier, I said that when I changed my awareness of myself from, I Am *a psychologist* to I Am *a problem solver who wants to have a positive impact in the world*, that switch opened up ways for me to be a problem solver in different industries and sectors with people, teams, executives, companies, organizations, and foundations.

After several years of being a practicing clinical psychologist, I took my talents and skills to work in a global research and best practices firm for companies and their executives. My first role was in new business development for corporate clientele.

You might be wondering (as many did) why a psychologist would consider making such a big move and whether it was a career drift versus a shift. But I was able to identify and use a few key transferrable skills that allowed me to make a smooth transition from being a practicing psychologist to working in corporate consultative sales.

Psychologists are known for being really good listeners. In fact, we call it being able to listen with the third ear; listening for the deeper layers in a conversation and hearing what is not being directly said. At the same time, what is usually the biggest complaint that people have with salespeople? The complaint is that they don't listen well because they are too busy trying to sell you on their product or service. I positioned myself when I made my career transition not just as a psychologist, but as the best listener they could ever hire. In case you want to know how that career shift turned out for me, I ended up setting a company record for how much business I generated in that year.

Every position I have held or created from my playbook since then has always been an offshoot of my key talents and skills I can transfer to seemingly very different kinds of experiences. And just as importantly, they all are ways for me gain experiences that help me move closer to my bigger vision.

⟨ MORE WAYS TO MAKE THE PLAYS ⟩

AFTER BROADENING YOUR VIEW of what you can do with your bigger *I Am*, and your predictable patterns, you can also broaden your sense of ways to make those plays.

Our traditional academic education mainly teaches us to think about and prepare for the traditional career ladder; preparing ourselves to have a job through an employer. But now there are more choices available to us. Aside from working inside an organization, there are various ways to be self-employed that allow you to leverage your assets and skills.

This move toward self-employment and more independent ways of working is nothing new, but it certainly received increased attention after the recession when more people had to put together a variety of work solutions—such as starting a personal business and doing freelance side gigs to stay afloat. The increased options that we have to enable us to take advantage of a few trends,[4] including the technology revolution, our more globalized and networked world, the rise in online platforms that allow people to connect with ease and the greater variety of E-Commerce marketplaces. Access to funding through creative online platforms have also brought the dream of starting a business within reach for so many who did not believe it was an option for them. Freelance work has given many the flexibility to set their own schedules, given them more control over their earning potential as well as helping them to cover their financial gaps.

But just as we have talked about the challenges associated with traditional career ladders, the rise in freelance and contract work is also not without its share of challenges. Unlike employer-based contracts, independent-work contracts do not provide traditional employment benefits such as health insurance and retirement benefits. When you take a vacation, since there is no paid time off, you are also taking a break from your income, and the inconsistent work and cash flow can be difficult to manage.

This underscores the point that there is no perfect one-size-fits-all solution for how we can or should work. The key is to broaden your understanding of the choices available to you and create a playbook with multiple options and paths that best suit you and play to your strengths.

Here are a few ways to leverage your skills and predictable patterns to create your own full-time, part-time, or side-gig options.

Service-Based Businesses

In service-based businesses, customers purchase your time and skills by engaging with you in a one-on-one relationship. Given all the available options, there is a wide range and level of skills you can monetize. The most basic example we all know is making extra money by just having a car and driving others around. But let's go further: If you have strong design skills, you can provide design services such as logos, signs, and web graphics for business customers. You could create a food catering business. You could create a painting service. If you are naturally detailed and organized, you might consider being a professional organizer. If you know a foreign language, you might consider being a translator. Maybe you are handy and can leverage your plumbing skills. You can also start a business based on your interests. For example, you might try pet sitting if you love pets.

Nancy's group of travelers quickly caught on to that concept. Roberta mentioned her love of working with kids and the possibility of starting a children's tutoring business. Shelly could use the marketing skills she now devoted to her employer and instead create her own marketing or public-relations agency. Bobby could create his own web-design company. Gina could create her own copywriting and editing service.

Consulting-Based Businesses

WITH A CONSULTING-BASED BUSINESS, like a service-based business, you have a direct relationship with your clients. However, with a consulting-based business, instead of providing a service, consultants and coaches leverage their expertise to help clients solve their problems and achieve their goals. For example, there are businesses built around the many issues we face such as general life coaches, career coaches, business consultants, nutrition coaches, transition coaches, personal-fitness coaches, and image consultants. Here again the level of expertise varies widely, from more general coaching to highly specialized consulting.

You might choose to work directly in a one-on-one relationship with people, but now with talent-on-demand on the rise within many companies, people are choosing to consult with organizations directly, as experts with more specialized skills that are then placed in temporary assignments inside those companies.

Again, the possibilities available through consulting caught the imagination of Nancy's travelers. With her marketing background, Shelly realized she could consider a becoming a marketing consultant to help businesses figure out the best marketing channels for their goals. With her social media expertise, Gina realized she could consider being a social media consultant. Roberta said she has considered being a career consultant. Bobby started to think about being a software consultant, and Mark, with his strong operations expertise thought about becoming a business-operations consultant.

While there are many advantages to creating either service-based and consulting-based businesses such as the close client connection, one drawback, however, is that you are trading dollars for hours since you are exchanging your time for money. There is also a limit on how many clients you can take on, since it is a one-on-one relationship. The good news is that there are also some great ways to use your skills while also *leveraging* your time, so let's look at a few of those.

Product-Based Businesses

PRODUCT-BASED BUSINESSES DELIVER PHYSICAL, tangible products. You can sell through your own online store or through other marketplaces, such as Amazon, eBay, and Etsy. You might want to create your own jewelry, then sell it online. You might design and sell your own clothing or other handmade crafts. You could consider creating monthly subscription boxes for toys, or items like hand-crafted soaps or products for morning rituals, like coffee and tea, or you might create subscription boxes around an eco-friendly lifestyle. As you brainstorm ideas for the kinds of products that you can sell, also remember to include thinking about your interests and what you like to do for fun, and using those as ways you might be able to create a living with your interests.

Information-Based Businesses

WHILE CONSULTANTS AND COACHES work one-on-one with their clients, information-based businesses allow you to share your expertise and information in ways that leverage your time. Like other skill- or expertise-based businesses, information-based businesses are aligned around a common problem, solution, audience, or message. (Please note that I am *not* referring to get-rich-quick marketers, products, or seminars). With these businesses, you are creating multiple ways to share information. For example, you can be an author, a blogger, or a podcaster. You can create a newsletter, an online course, or a series of YouTube videos or webinars to share your expertise with others. If you can identify a need and fill it, the possibilities are almost endless.

Small Businesses

WITH MOST OF THE kinds of businesses we discussed, you can work out of your home or rent space elsewhere. You are also the business. It is your time, your products, your expertise, you are either trading or leveraging. When you disappear, so does the business. Another option is to not just create a job for yourself but to instead create a business with systems, processes, and staff in place to deliver a product or service. When you think of the corner convenience store, the local coffee shop, your hairdresser, the flower shop, these are all everyday examples of small businesses.

One important distinction to keep in mind as you consider your options is that while there are many positive reasons to either create a small business or grow your current business into one, a trap many business owners fall into when starting a small business is what Michael Gerber describes as not realizing you need to switch your perspective from working *in* your business to working *on* it.

Consider the fact that many arrived at starting their own business accidentally, especially right after the economic downturn. Meaning, they did not necessarily set out to work for themselves. Perhaps they were downsized and needed to fill financial gaps, or they realized they wanted to take more control of their financial future. They took their talents and created a job for themselves, by just transferring their key skills from working for someone else to working for themselves. However, as their business started to grow, the next logical step seemed to be taking on other employees or contractors, and creating a small business.

What they usually did not consider, however is that doing so also meant needing to steer the ship, as well as oversee key business components such as sales and marketing, technology, staffing and management, the finances, and tax compliance to name a few.

Now, before we go any further, think back to the series questions you answered to help you discover your predictable patterns. One question, in particular, asked you about what perspective you like to take on teams such as the visionary, the translator, the people developer, the implementer, or the researcher. If you are someone who is more inclined to be the big picture person, then taking on more of a visionary, direction-setting, and leadership role that a small business requires, rather than doing all of the direct client work and getting bogged down in the day-to-day tasks that you would have also had to do if you were working by yourself might sound exciting. If you prefer to be the person that manages and keeps track of all of the moving parts, connecting all the pieces together, then taking on that kind of role in your small business might also seem exciting to you. If, however, you only get excited by the direct client work; then you will likely struggle with transitioning from working in your business to working on it. It might be more difficult for you to let go some of the direct the day-to-day client work that energizes you, and trade that for tasks that frankly do not excite you. Ofttimes, small business owners don't realize what they truly got themselves into, because the opportunity to make more revenue always sounds like a good thing. This is where though, it is critical to know how to hire well to build a team around you that can also fill in the gaps in a way that keeps everyone in their talents, strengths, skills and predictable styles and patterns.

Working Inside a Company

THE IMPORTANCE OF KNOWING what value you add and using it to your advantage is not just for those who are self-employed. If you work for an employer, you should always see yourself as an intrapreneur. An intrapreneur is a someone who adopts the same mindset as entrepreneurs, but the difference is they work inside an organization, not for themselves. Intrapreneurs try to make themselves invaluable by constantly identifying gaps, looking for opportunities, and finding ways to innovate inside their organization.

As you think about ways to create more plays inside an organization, be careful of falling in the same mindset trap that we just described that many small business owners fall into. The path up the traditional career ladder is typically one where you begin as an individual contributor. Once you are able to demonstrate your skills and abilities as an individual contributor, then the "reward" is usually being groomed or considered for positions in management, where similar to what we just described, you are no longer as close to the direct client work or product creation, and you are more involved in the management of people, and even the oversight of broader pieces of the business with greater career progression.

I cannot begin to tell you though, how many executives I have coached who were in career crisis either because of the Peter Principle and/or general disengagement with their new roles one they got promoted. The Peter Principle is the observation that in most organizational hierarchies, employees will keep climbing the company ladder and continue to be promoted until they are promoted out of their area of competence.

Here is a very common reason why this happens. Once again, think back to our questions on predictable talents, strengths, and predictable perspectives that we like to take on teams. If you start off as a very strong individual contributor, and in fact, you do not do as well in more team, and collaborative roles, then it is essentially a career killer to "promote" such people into management positions, as is often the case. These people intuitively also know these are not the best roles for them, but since the positions come with more money, prestige, etc. attached to it, it is very hard to turn down. As we said earlier, more money always sounds like a good thing. This circumstance, unfortunately often leads to people being promoted *up* then *out* because of the bad person-role fit unless it is fixed somehow. But if you think about it, their skills did not change. What did change, however was what was being asked of them.

The Power of Choice

As you consider all the ways you can make a play, the important idea in this early stage of creating your playbook is that as you brainstorm your list of plays, you want to stack the deck in your favor with as many good choices as possible that make sense for you. Keep certain things in mind, like how close you want to stay to the client work versus how much you want to leverage your skills and create a system and business. Think about how much you want to work by yourself versus how much you want to work with others. Do you like working online, in person with clients, or at a brick-and-mortar business? The key is to use your goals and predictable patterns and map them to the kinds of plays that you can best use to your advantage.

The Gut-Punch Rule

As you are brainstorming all the things you can do, you should also know your deal-breakers. In other words, you should have a good sense of what is *not* you. You should know what you cannot do and what you just can't live with. These are more than just getting outside your comfort zone. These are things that are so far outside of who you are, that when you consider them, it feels like you have just been punched in the gut.

Here are some examples of gut punchers:

- I simply cannot give away my talents and skills in service of someone else's dream.
- My deal breaker is the idea of anyone having the power to hold me back.
- I can't work for a place that does not have a mission I care about.
- It's soul sucking to me to wake up knowing I have to go to work and distract myself just to try to get through another day.
- I can't live a nine-to-five lifestyle.
- The idea of not having a regular paycheck punches me in the gut.
- Working for myself and by myself is just not me; I need to have someplace to go with structured responsibilities each day.
- I would rather work eighty hours a week for myself than forty for someone else.
- I can't imagine myself without a benefits package.

The Essential You

As we've learned, creating our own career playbook means that we need to approach our life from the top down instead of from the bottom up. In other words, rather than defining ourselves by our degree and our job titles only, we must now approach our careers from the top down, meaning, from the things that are most true and unfiltered about us (what we really care about deeply), to how we manifest that on a daily basis, and what plays we can make based on our talents, skills, and predictable patterns. Approaching our life this top-down way ensures that we can build our playbook in a way that is consistent with our *Essential You*.

- My compass and my clocks
- My *why*
- Predictable patterns of my assets
- Sectors, populations, and my interests

Now, it's your turn to brainstorm and get as many ideas as possible of the kinds of plays you are interested in making, and the ways you can make them for your playbook. Be creative. You can look at career listings sites, talk to people, and tap into your networks, to expose yourself to the many options that may be a good fit for you and your bigger vision.

Step Three: How to Stand Apart

When you don't know who you are, others will always be willing to decide on your behalf.

—Dr. Natalia Peart

Now THAT YOU HAVE some success markers on your wall and a playbook with many possible plays you can make, it's now time to figure out how to create your own footholds to give yourself a leg up in a competitive environment.

Your Unique Advantage

THE FIRST STEP IS knowing how to play to your advantage. So far, you have created your playbook based on what you care deeply about and your *why* (your compass), the effortless actions that keep you in the zone (clocks), and your other predictable patterns you can use to your advantage.

While your playbook helps you identify many ways you can reach your goal and hedge against risk by opening up many more choices right from the start, only some of those plays might position you to truly stand apart by giving you a unique advantage.

This next step we are going to learn is critical, because often times we stop at just the level of knowing our predictable patterns of talents and strengths, which is good but not good enough. To position yourself for continued success even in the midst of uncertainty, you need to take it up a notch and create strong footholds that help you stack the deck in your favor.

There are two things you must know to find your "unique advantage."

First, you need to understand what is most *unique* about you. Even beyond your talents and strengths, your *gifts* are the highest expression of your uniqueness. Gifts are an exceptional talent or natural ability that makes you stand above all the rest. They are usually closely tied to what you care deeply about and/or to something you believe you were created to do. When you think about the feedback you consistently receive, when do you think you shine the brightest?

Take a moment to write down what you think is *most* unique about you, or your gift.

———————————————————————————

———————————————————————————

———————————————————————————

———————————————————————————

Second, you need to know your *advantage* in the marketplace. To identify your advantage, you will need to shift your perspective by stepping outside yourself and seeing what gaps, challenges, and problems in your company, for your clients, or in the world do you help address or even solve. To do that, think carefully about all of the opportunities you have had so far in your career, and also think ahead to your bigger vision and what you care about deeply, and ask yourself: *What value do I produce, add, or create for others?*

This is important because by knowing what needs you can uniquely and specifically address, and what you do that other people need, you will also know *how to align what you do best with what people actually value and need.*

Here are the two extremes that we can experience when what we do best is not aligned with what other people need.

On one extreme, the situation many people face right now is that when they work for their employer, their employer must take their gifts, talents, skills and *translate* what they bring in a way that allows the employer to meet their customers' needs.

That translation is their job description. If people are fortunate enough to have a job description that matches most of their gifts and talents and their *why*, with what their company needs, they have a great job fit and will likely feel highly engaged in what they do. Oftentimes, though, people find themselves using their skills in ways that benefit their employer while they themselves are left feeling disengaged from their jobs every day because they are not moving closer to their bigger vision, or applying their gifts and talents in ways that they would like.

There is however, another guardrail you should avoid hitting. People who are looking to make life changes are often told, "Follow your passion." The problem is, that's incomplete advice because what you are passionate about may not be something others need and that allows you to add value in the marketplace. When that happens, you have created something you love to do, but it may just end up being a great hobby. There is nothing wrong with creating a great hobby, of course, if that is your intention.

To create something meaningful to you, but also valuable to others, you must align some of the plays in your playbook with your ability to uniquely add value if you want to create strong footholds for your journey.

Understanding what value you currently add or can add requires that you truly understand and empathize with the needs of the people, populations, and potential customers you care about, or know the big gaps inside of your company. In other words, you must be able to understand *their* experiences and motivations—*not just yours*—to make sure you have a deep understanding of the issues and potential gaps you can fill.

To empathize, you may need to make a few observations of people interacting with a product or service so you can unobtrusively get a sense of the pain points, or you may need to conduct interviews, hold focus groups, and/or find other creative ways to gain a deeper understanding of potential problems and needs.

> **Empathize**
>
> To *empathize* is to lay aside your own assumptions by gaining direct insight into others' needs and the problems you want to solve.

Now, create a list of the needs of the people, populations, and potential customers you care about or if you are employed by someone else, some of the current gaps currently being experienced in their process or service. Narrow down the list of the problems they face to those that *you are uniquely positioned to help address*, especially when you consider your bigger vision.

Notice again that your unique advantage should have both internal value for you—a way to get to meaningful action that ideally uses your gifts. But it should also have external value—it should help address a need. The question you must ask yourself here is *what is a significant need in the marketplace right now that I can fill in a way that also moves me forward on my compass goals?*

Here is my own example to help illustrate how this works. When looking at what stands out as my gift, I noticed that regardless of where I worked and how I worked, I was particularly gifted at helping people, teams, companies, and organizations not just manage change but also helping them create new directions and futures. I am therefore not just a problem solver; I am a change expert.

This method of finding your unique advantage helps you move from a list of potential plays in your playbook you can make, to knowing how you *add unique value* to others. It also moves you closer to your bigger vision in a way that helps you stand apart from others and remain relevant even in constantly changing conditions.

Like all the other lists you've been brainstorming, this exercise is not a one-and-done. You need to create a habit of constantly paying attention to the new and evolving needs in the market that you can address—ideally as uniquely as possible. This constant scanning will help you make sure you always stay relevant, since you will always want know how to evolve your value no matter what is happening around you.

What You Stand For

Do you know what you stand for?

Just as your internal compass helps guide what you *choose* to do, your core values help define the boundaries of what you *should* and should not do. In other words, we all need to know what we stand for—our code, our fiber, our personal boundaries. Our core values are the way we orient ourselves to the world and how we express what we think is most important to us as a human being. Our values transcend context because they are based on what is important to us.

These are so central to us that when we're not aligned with our core values, we experience internal conflict. They resonate so intensely with us that we simply know they are us. We feel them deeply and passionately, and we want to live and act in ways that integrate our values into our life as part of who we are. They help us to make critical decisions and to feel more centered and grounded.

We've all heard stories of people who lose their way because their talents and skills write a check their character just can't cash. That happens because they were not rooted in core values and enduring principles to guide their decision-making. Developing strong core values is what helps us firmly plant our feet in our footholds during our journey, and it's what helps to steady us regardless of what else is happening around us.

There are many possible core values to consider, but Nancy asked the travelers to brainstorm a few that may be the most important for them.

- honesty
- integrity
- trustworthiness
- kindness
- love
- mastery
- curiosity
- wisdom
- freedom
- courage
- contribution
- service
- fairness
- unity
- perseverance
- equality
- gratitude

Knowing both how you stand apart and what you stand for, together help you bring your full self into clear alignment with the outside world. It is what provides the footholds and the positioning that will help you make your climb even steadier.

Step Four: Connect Your Plays

THE TRADITIONAL CAREERS LADDERS we were used to navigating before had clear rungs and connections that made the climb more predictable. In other words, when we worked for a company, there was usually a clear career progression that took you from entry level to higher levels of responsibility. Because our climb is no longer based on one clear job ladder for a job that we are expected to hold for life, and instead it is based on different plays that may or may not be as naturally connected, we sometimes need to connect our plays by creating our own bridges and transitions. These connections are what help us keep our footing even when we are piecing together plays so we don't fall through the gaps between our plays. They also help us keep different kinds of plays running at the same time, which again helps us hedge against risk if one path unexpectedly ends or requires a detour.

Some of the plays you use will be your *main plays*; the ones meant to move you toward your bigger compass goals and that also allow you to track your progress against your success markers. These main plays are ideally also using your unique advantage you have identified so that you are connected to both what you want and ways to create value in the marketplace.

Side plays, or gigs, can serve many functions in your journey. They are now becoming more common, and according to a Bankrate survey,[5] nearly four of every ten people (37 percent) have a side job. Side plays can help you shore up or build your financial resources since they are often meant to help you plug the gaps in your expenses or build your resources for funding your dream. Side plays can also help you transition, or bridge, more smoothly from a full-time job with an employer to self-employment without the risk of completely losing your salary and benefits all at once. For example, you may need to first find ways to work in the evenings and on the weekends to build up your new main play before you give up your previous main job.

Some plays that you make may help you rebuild completely after a setback. For example, it may be that you have experienced a sudden drop in income, or some other emergency or disaster, and now you need to take a time-out, stop the financial bleeding, sell assets, or move in with other family members among other scenarios, in order to regroup.

It's common to feel like you're wasting time or wandering off the path when you're not making a main play. But these connector plays are also important, even if they are not your main play. As long as you can connect what you're doing with your bigger picture, you know why you're doing what you're doing, and you know what purpose your current play serves, it won't feel so wasted or meaningless.

You will always face some creative constraints when it's time to make your plays. For example, sometimes family obligations limit what you can do and when. Just remember, even though there may be constraints on your time and/ or money, you are always in the driver's seat if you know the big picture of where you want to go.

We can't wait for perfect conditions before we act. In fact, now we have to expect to take steps and move forward in uncertain or less than optimal or conditions. Embrace the constraints and rethink how you must do things to come up with innovative solutions to move around your constraints and use different plays that can help you get it done.

Again, there is no one right combination of plays. It is about what is right for you. Just remember that each play you make must help you make strides toward your bigger vision while helping you hedge against the constant change that we now experience. In deciding what plays to choose and when, make sure that you know what your choices are and when each might be helpful to you. Know that regardless of what plays you choose, you can run more than one play at the same time to smooth your transitions and help you move further toward your goals.

Step Five: From a Playbook to a System of Success

Now that you have a good set of possible plays and ways to connect them, it's time to make some choices out of the possibilities in your playbook, that will move you forward. To do so, you will consider all your goals and current circumstances, and figure out which plays you want to prototype.

Prototype

To *prototype* is to create scaled-down solutions that better help you investigate your plays.

The reason you want to prototype first and not just go full steam ahead on everything you are possibly considering, is that the time, money, and opportunity costs are too great for you to just try to run every play you are considering even before you get some indication of whether it is worth it.

To prototype well, make sure you are leveraging the people, networks, and systems all around you. To go from lots of plays to creating a system of success is the difference between simple and compound interest. When you are earning simple interest, it is only based on the original dollars you invested, or the original principal. If you are earning compound interest, you are not only earning interest on the original principal, but you are also earning interest on the interest. When you are able to not just use the power of what you can do, but also *leverage* the power of what others can do on your behalf, that is taking your playbook from a series of plays, to a more powerful system than you can create on our own.

Your goal is to go from a playbook of plays to a *system of success* that will get you where you want to be more quickly by leveraging other people's knowledge, connections, and influence so that you can progress a lot quicker and further than you ever could have on your own. That means you must constantly position yourself to not just build skills and experiences but also build the support and teams that will help guide, bridge, or broaden your view of new plays you can make, open new opportunities, advocate on your behalf, and steer you away from any potential pitfalls. Your network can help you see, hear, and extend your reach in ways you'd never be able to on your own. This leverage also helps your journey feel more secure and manageable.

To grow your network, you need to build your weak ties as well your strong ones. The difference between a strong and a weak network tie is both important and counterintuitive.

A *strong network tie* is someone you know well. Typically, strong ties will provide you with a sense of support, comfort, companionship, and belonging. They also tend to know the same people and information you know. These are people like your friends and family. They support you, encourage you, help build your confidence, and are essential for your sense of connection and overall well-being.

Weak network ties, on the other hand, are people you don't know well; you may have different interests, and you probably don't interact much. They are often a friend of a friend, and therefore you are loosely connected to them through one or two degrees of separation. But make no mistake, while weak ties are usually activated only for a specific purpose, their power is anything but weak. These ties are crucial in connecting you to new relationships and networks. They are usually the ones well positioned to help you connect to more plays because they extend your reach beyond your current circle and networks of the people you already know.

Both weak and strong ties can provide information about the possible paths you are considering. You do not have to go down every road yourself. You can learn from the experiences of those who have been there before you. These people can open you up to opportunities you were unaware of; they can also help you make the connections needed for your next step.

If you're curious about a certain industry, ask yourself if you know anyone who could help connect you. Are you part of networking groups that broaden your reach on a regular basis? Can you shadow people, or find a way to experience "a day in the life," that will expose you to what they do and how they do it so you can see if it is a good match for you? That's why it's important to diversify your networks and expand the people with whom you connect. You need more than your family, your friends, and the people in your current field. Strong ties can help support you, but weak ties are an essential bridge to new information.

You should also look for professional mentors who can advise you and sponsors who can advocate for you. Don't make the mistake of thinking your journey is just about your competency. That is the fallacy of one. You need to keep nurturing these kinds of relationships all along the way.

Overall, going from a playbook to a system of success helps you move from what feels like a steep climb on your own to a more manageable walk up the ramp with the help of others.

Step Six: Manage Your Portfolio of Experiences

Do the best you can until you know better. Then when you know better, do better.

—Dr. Maya Angelou

Once you've prototyped and tested the plays you've chosen, you need to then ask yourself what feedback you are getting, how are you growing, and what you are learning about yourself in all these experiences that can help you move forward and stay on track toward your eventual career goals.

> ## Test
>
> When you *test* your prototypes, you determine how well they solve the problem, which helps you make further refinements.

WHEN YOU MAKE YOUR plays, what feedback are you getting about your big goals? Does the feedback make your path any clearer? Does it help you refine your bigger vision by seeing more patterns in what you choose and don't choose? Does it add more information? What are you learning about the things that are missing in your plays and/or your skills? What must you grow?

You need to maintain a Success Portfolio™ for your plays so you can ask yourself these kinds of critical questions about all your experiences. Make sure all your plays are in your portfolio so you can track what those plays are contributing to your big goals based on where you really want to go and your success markers. If you don't track your feedback and adjust your plays accordingly, you'll simply drift from one thing to the next with no big picture tying it all together. Again, this is the big difference between just drifting along versus shifting and adjusting your plays based on feedback or changing external conditions.

This feedback should constantly help you figure out what you need to start doing next, what you are currently doing that you need to continue doing in order to grow, what you should stop doing, and what you need to adjust.

If you are working for someone else but you already know that your job is not a part of your eventual goal, it is especially important to make sure you are answering these kinds of key portfolio questions every six months. While you should always be in the job market informally by being open to new opportunities, regularly managing your portfolio also reduces the risk of you allowing yourself and your career to drift by letting someone else control your journey.

Beyond the all-important paycheck, is your job providing you with the skills, networks, and or experiences that you need to leverage, start, or grow? Are you just killing time and just doing busywork? Is it providing the kind of financial resources that you need?

Ask yourself if there are key skills you need to develop that you are missing. Are there key experiences in your company that would be helpful to have? Can you negotiate to get those experiences? Do not be afraid to not only *highlight* the value that you provide, but to also *negotiate* for the salary and key learning experiences that are important for you to continue to grow. Your boss shouldn't be the only one who decides when your time is up. There is no shame or stigma attached to saying it's time to leave, especially if the job is not your ultimate goal.

Regardless of which plays you're making, always know why you're making them and how long you plan to make them based on the feedback you are receiving and how you need to manage and adjust your portfolio. Knowing this keeps you in control instead of letting someone else control your situation. More steps on your journey will show up once you step forward, prototype, and get feedback. You should always keep a few things in play. Some will work, and some will not. Learn and iterate. How you choose, how you sort, and how you determine the things that are not you is a constant process, including what you need to do right now to navigate the open waters.

As you execute, you will start to see which plays are working and which ones seemed promising but ultimately are not as successful perhaps due to changing conditions or new constraints that you need to work around. The advantage of having a playbook with a few possible plays, is that you will always have other options that you can choose. You can then integrate what you learn and refine your next set of plays. Some potential paths and plays will not even come into view unless you take a step forward, so you always need to have a bias toward acting even in uncertainty.

You will find that you will need to work outside your comfort zone to make moves even when you don't feel ready. You'll also need to be flexible so you can adjust based on what you're learning.

In order to be able to take advantage of what is in your playbook, you need to be constantly evolving your skills and keeping up with the trends to make sure that you are able to spot and take advantage of continual opportunities as they arise. Make sure that you are developing the kinds of skills that we all need, regardless of whether you work for yourself or someone else, in order to stay competitive. Skills such as critical thinking, problem solving, adaptability, collaboration, and communication, are some of the key twenty-first century skills we should all master.

Many online learning platforms are available today that put almost anything you want to know and learn more about—personally or professionally—right at your fingertips. You should always be thinking about ways to invest in yourself.

We used to debate whether it was better to be a generalist or a specialist in your approach to your career, meaning, we used to ask whether it was better to develop a broad "jack of all trades" knowledge base that you could apply more widely, or develop a specific expertise that allowed you to specialize and apply your skills more deeply. Rather than approaching this issue of how to develop your skills as an either/ or question, you should now see yourself as needing to be both a generalist and a specialist by developing your skills to be "T" shaped. Being "T" shaped means that not only do you have the depth of expertise in one area, but also, you are able to move across different fields and disciplines by applying your knowledge more broadly.

As with everything else, managing your portfolio is not a one-and-done process. Develop the habit of constantly refining your portfolio based on feedback so you never lose sight of your bigger vision no matter how many plays it takes, or the disruptions along the way.

Manage Your Portfolio of Experiences

WHEN YOU DECIDE ON your path, you should also know:

1. What you need:
   - What kinds of experiences?
   - What skills?
   - What financial resources?
   - What other resources, such as contacts, networks, mentorship?

2. For each experience, evaluate:
   - What did I love?
   - What was I best at?
   - What did I hate?

3. When you work for someone else, ask:
   - Do I hope this is my final stop?
   - What is missing from this experience, and can I get it here?
   - When will it be time to move on?

Step Seven: Tell Your Own Story

As YOU LOOK AT your climbing walls, your journey and plays will make sense to you, but they may not make sense to an outside observer. That's why your last step is to translate your path and tell your story in a way that makes sense to others.

Storytelling

Storytelling is an essential human activity for sharing experiences. The "through line" is the driving force and thread that binds your story together.

Your story's through line brings coherence to your story of yourself. When you are creating your journey, your job title is no longer what holds it together—it's your through line, your *why*. It is the way to tell your story to others so it hangs together no matter how scattered the plays may seem on the surface. The through line is what helps you to effectively connect the dots of your own journey.

As the boss of your own career, you also need to be comfortable with the fact that now being the holder of your own value and not waiting for others to decide your value, also means knowing how to communicate your story effectively to others. For many, I know this this brings up a sense of discomfort because you were taught or learned that it was better to be humble. The truth is, it is simply not an option to just wait for someone to see your value–you must be willing to see it first and communicate it.

As you present your story of yourself to others—perhaps in a re-sume—you should tell a compelling story of your unique advantage, your transferrable skills, and then use the more traditional listing of roles you have occupied as examples of your compelling story of yourself.

There are numerous ways to tie your story together. Here are some common through lines:

1. A major event in your life that serves like a before-and-after. The reason for a major pivot, like a death, a loss, or a broader issue that suddenly surfaces and really stirs you.
2. The creativity/innovation you consistently exhibit regardless of context.
3. A problem you want to solve regardless of how and where you solve it.
4. Your desire to help empower others.
5. A gift you have used in various situations.
6. Your leadership abilities in various situations and environments.
7. A broader issue you care about and how your work connects to that bigger mission.

This is just a sampling of different ways to tell your story and connect the pieces with a through line.

Like everything else, this is an iterative, not a one-and-done process. You need to build lifelong habits of constantly growing your portfolio and telling your story. The more you figure out what you've learned from your experiences, the clearer you will be on your story and where you're trying to go. This process is not a straight line—it is much more flexible and nonlinear.[6]

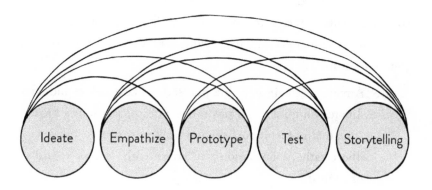

When the day was done, Nancy asked the travelers to take some time to reflect on anything they wanted to write about. As they left the climbing walls, they couldn't wait to go back, have dinner, and chat about their day. They knew they had not yet completed the journey, but they were excited by all they had learned so far and were eager to start journaling whatever came to mind.

HABIT THREE

THE NEW MENTAL FITNESS

Our Self-Talk

THIS MORNING, UNLIKE THE previous mornings, when the travelers met for breakfast, they were noticeably quiet and more tentative. They decided to skip their usual morning chat and instead sat quietly before it was time to get started. As they walked into the room, some even looked deflated. They sat and quietly waited until Nancy asked them to share the thoughts they had written in their journals.

Gina expressed worry that what she was planning to do had already been done by lots of other people, so she was no longer sure it was a good idea. She started thinking about working for herself, but she didn't feel confident she even knew how to get started. She worried she didn't have enough money and that maybe she hadn't learned enough yet. Though starting her own business was something she wanted when she first came on this journey, now she was not so sure.

Roberta journaled about the things going on in her life right now, and that she was not sure she'd be able to find the time to make some of the changes she'd planned. With all she had going on at home, she worried that this might not be the right time for her to take her career in a new direction. While she was journaling, her stress increased so much she wasn't sure she wanted to continue the journey.

Bobby started thinking about his big vision but got overwhelmed when he realized how many pieces of the process he was still missing. He was worried about not having any networks or connections that could help him and about not knowing anyone who'd done what he wanted to do. As he journaled, he started to feel intimidated.

Shelly brought with her the business plan she'd created a few years ago. As she started going over it again last night, she wrote that she was worried about unwinding her life. She got very distracted from journaling by thinking about her new project at work. Every time she started reading through the old business plan, she started to feel very uncomfortable because it reminded her that she'd already tried to start her business once before and hadn't followed through.

Mark found it very hard to journal anything: each time he tried, he started reflecting on times when he felt good about himself. He thought about what his old job and old life meant to him, and what he no longer had. The only thing he wrote in his journal was about some of his worries about his financial obligations.

They all agreed that yesterday, they left feeling energized and ready to take on the world, but by the time they were ready to come back today, they felt stuck again. They were even starting to wonder if they had gone backward instead of forward.

Here is more of what they wrote:

- I'm too old.
- My many current obligations are holding me back.
- I don't have enough money.

- To start my business, I would have to ask people for money, and I don't like to do that.
- I don't have enough experience.
- I should've gotten a different degree.
- My skills are outdated.
- I don't know anyone who can help me.
- I'm scared.

Shelly spoke up. "No matter how far I go, I always end up here. I have been going around in circles for a while. I'm hopeful, then I'm defeated. Time is running out. Can someone please tell me what to do?"

They all waited in silence, hoping for Nancy to give words of comfort, motivation, or to say anything, really, but instead she simply said, "Okay, *now* it's time to go."

Go where?

⟨ BENEATH THE SURFACE ⟩

THE DAY'S JOURNEY BEGAN on a ship. Nancy explained, "Yesterday we learned how to make the career plays we need for our journey in today's world; now it's time to learn the life-navigation skills you need to actually make it happen. In the past, we assumed our academic and career skills were enough for success. We assumed those skills alone made us fit enough to be successful."

Nancy explained that change was happening at a more rapid pace than ever before, and they couldn't just ignore it. "We need to have the mental tools—the mental fitness—to navigate our new world. What is different now is that constant change, with its resulting stress and anxiety, is now part of the backdrop of our lives. We don't want the constant change and the stress to shut us down. Instead, we need to learn not only how to be resilient in the face of change but also learn the skills that will help us be agile so we can constantly make new plays and thrive despite the challenges change can pose. With all you've learned, you know how to create your playbook. But you don't yet have the life skills you need to make those plays. It's time to start learning those skills."

As the ship sailed, Nancy asked the travelers to take a look at an iceberg in the waters ahead. "During the last several days, you've learned how to take a top-down approach to your life," she reminded them. "Today's view will be from the bottom up—the journey will begin deep inside you, since most of your life-navigation skills are largely beneath the surface and mostly unseen, just like this iceberg. Today's journey is going to start at the bottom, because that's where all the action is. It's time to look beneath the surface."

There's Resistance...

We don't see things as they are, we see things as we are.

—Rabbi Shemuel ben Nachmani

Your Predictable Patterns

SO FAR, WE'VE LEARNED about the power of knowing our predictable patterns. I call it power because knowing our patterns, as we saw, helps us figure out how we can use those patterns to our advantage. Just as with the *why* behind your big-vision goal, your gifts, talents, strengths, and working style all have predictable patterns, so does your response to change. And in this case, it's important to know your patterns of how you typically respond to change because in times of disruptive change and the stress it causes, we lean on our predictable patterns of how we respond to change much more than we realize. It's probably only partially in your awareness right now, but once you bring your style to the surface, in other words, to your attention, you can better see what is working against you when you're trying to grow.

The bottom line about change, whether it is something we want or not, is that change can be stressful. And just like other predictable patterns, we all have a predictable relationship with change.

Some people are *Wave Creators*, who not only embrace change but seek out opportunities to make the necessary course corrections to follow their own path or adapt very quickly to sudden or unexpected situations. They move confidently toward what is ahead despite the uncertainties. In other words, they *lean* into the waves of change, and they can even become excited by the very idea of big and innovative changes.

A second group are *Wave Riders,* or those who are not necessarily leading the changes, but they can and will, with some guidance, adapt to their circumstances and ride the wave to wherever they must go. Even though they may initially be overwhelmed by the thought of change, these are people who can adapt rather than be stymied by the change. While it may take this group some time to warm up to a new idea, with some reflection, they can get on board as long as it is logical and they can visualize the results of their efforts.

A third group are *Wave Resisters,* or those who instinctively want to hang back on the shore and wait until it is over. The will often say "But this is the way we've always done it in the past." In other words, they are unwilling to lose sight of the shore. It doesn't matter if hanging out on the shore is to their detriment. They will do it as they've always known it or as they've always seen it because they are so gripped by what feels comfortable and familiar to them. They are not going anywhere or doing anything differently.

The truth is, most people are either Wave Riders or Wave Resisters and are therefore motivated by the avoidance of the pain of change as opposed to the goal they want to reach. This is critical to understand, because while most of us can identify that we want something more in our life, we are likely more motivated to avoid the uncertainty that change will bring to our life than to embrace the potential benefits of the changes we want. So instead, for many of us, the pain of staying the same has to get completely intolerable before we will act. We need our circumstances to completely fall apart around us before we will act. We will ignore what we know inside our knower, and we will choose to not to read the handwriting on the wall when it begins to appear that things are changing, since it will often take us to a place we are not ready to go.

And Then There's Resistance

THE TRAVELERS NOW APPROACH an iceboat and get in. The iceboat takes them deep beneath the surface of the iceberg.

The Story We Tell Ourselves

THE STORY WE TELL ourselves about ourselves is the most important story there is. The reason stories are important is because they help us make sense of our lives and experiences. They help us define who we are and shape how we think, what we believe, the choices we make, and the actions we take. Our stories either empower or limit us.

So the question is, does your story of yourself limit you from creating a new future, or does it fuel your growth? Sometimes when we are trying to change or rise higher in our lives, the story we're telling ourselves deep beneath the surface is actually limiting us.

Self-Knowledge:
Predictable Patterns

Self-Concept
Self-Confidence
Self-Worth

Self-Concept is how you define yourself. Your beliefs about who you are (*I Am*).

Self-Confidence is a belief that you can accomplish what you want (*I Can*).

Self-Worth is how you feel about yourself.

Whatever Follows I Am *Follows You*

"Now, LET'S GO DEEPER to where your *I Am* and *I Can* sit inside you." Nancy said to the group, "Do you remember when we were learning how to make our playbooks, we discussed how some people define their *I Am* by their job title, but that view was too narrow? We all found our bigger *I Am*, the aspirational *I Am* that is above the surface rooted in our big *why*." The travelers all said yes.

"Great, but that is not what I am referring to here. I am referring to a different *I Am* entirely—one that sits beneath the surface but is leading your journey without you even knowing it. What I am talking about are the *I Ams*, the limiting stories that have been running subconsciously in your head since you were very young. They sit so deeply within you that you've become oblivious to the power of those beliefs and how they run your life.

"Think of it this way. What's above the surface, what you're very conscious of, is governed by your rider[1]—the part of you that is rational, the part of you that created that aspirational, bigger vision of yourself we've been talking about for the past couple days. But it is the elephant that governs what sits beneath the surface; the things that are not in your conscious awareness, but direct you and you don't even realize it."

In a fight between your elephant and your rider, your elephant wins.

The rider, your conscious desires, thinks it is in charge, but whenever you kick up your higher-level desires, your elephant begins to pull you back down to your limiting beliefs.

Why is this? Why is our elephant so powerful?

According to Drs. Pratt and Lambrou,[2] our conscious mind includes our intellect, our ability to reason, our thoughts, and our future plans. But just like this iceberg that we see, our conscious mind, what is above the surface, represents only a tiny portion of our brain's capacity. What is the rest? The rest is our subconscious, or all the things below our level of awareness. Unlike the conscious mind, the subconscious mind also works largely by association. In other words, when we have an experience in our conscious awareness, our subconscious mind is looking for past experiences familiar to it, searching for information that helps us make sense of the current experience. Your subconscious automatically reacts to situations with its previously stored responses, and more and more evidence suggests that this happens quicker, and without the knowledge or control of your conscious mind.[3]

From a survival standpoint, this big difference in how fast our subconscious works was extremely adaptive. If, for example, we were in danger of being attacked by hungry lions, having our subconscious mind work quickly to *associate*, not *reason*, the smells, sights, and sounds that were familiar to a past experience was critical for our survival.

But here is where it all goes wrong.

What we also store from our past are the experiences that shape how we see ourselves and the meaning we have made of those experiences, true or not.

How do we develop negative, limiting beliefs?

When we come into this world, we're beings full of possibility. But as we grow, we often receive limiting messages from the world that shape who we are or who we think we should be. The main source of this information comes from family, peers, and from broader society. And even though most of these beliefs have nothing to do with who we actually are, what we're told and how it makes us feel all become seared into our subconscious because we experience these beliefs *as if* they were true. We also know that traumatic, stressful experiences are stored and recalled in our brain long after the event.[4] For instance, we all remember where we were on September 11, 2001, but not on September 10th.

Our limiting beliefs, like other traumatic events, are stored in our brain, and continue to be experienced as real and as true to us as when we had to protect ourselves from hungry lions. Every time we are in situations we can associate with those limiting beliefs, the elephant in us kicks up the negative self-talk that "protects" us but also holds us back.

The kinds of limiting beliefs we hold about ourselves are things like "I'm not smart enough," "I'm not powerful enough," "I'm not beautiful enough," "I'm not lovable enough," "I'm not worthy enough." Essentially, we don't believe we are enough. Because our subconscious mind can be much quicker and more powerful than our conscious mind, these beliefs end up shaping how we live our life.

It is no wonder that if what you consciously perceive (your rider) and your subconscious thoughts (your elephant) are not in alignment, your elephant will win, because of the power of your subconscious beliefs versus what you consciously believe or desire.

Nancy explained to the group that when they all left the journey yesterday excited about all the ways they were going to move *toward* what they desired, instead, what took over were all the limiting beliefs that ran in the background in their lives.

"When you think you are just trying to figure out the new plays of how to get to your life's sweet spot—what you deeply desire—think again," she said. "What you are also fighting against are the beliefs—the limiting beliefs from your elephant sitting here below."

"Your negative self-talk, the resistance that kicks up whenever your rider is taking you someplace your elephant doesn't believe you should go, is the reason you came back this morning feeling so exhausted and weighed down. Your rider is ready for you to kick into high gear, but your elephant is telling you that since you are not smart enough, powerful enough, worthy enough, or simply enough, it wants you to stay where you are and cling to the things your elephant has falsely told you that you need to be enough.

Your elephant wants you to cling to things like the trappings of your success, or the false image that others have of you, or needing the approval of others, or other symbols of status, because the story your elephant is telling you about yourself is that you are not enough without those things.

Even When You Get to Happy

You never rise higher than what you believe.
— *Dr. Natalia Peart*

NANCY CONTINUED. "LET'S THINK back for a moment to the first journey we took. Remember when we went down the first path to success that was on a permanent detour and we talked about why we never get to happy? Anyone notice that the higher you're looking to reach in your life, the louder the negative self-talk becomes and the more tired and exhausted you feel? It's not a coincidence. Here's how powerful it is. Even when you start to gain some success, the same insecurities you felt when you first started and that you thought were behind you once you become more successful, just keep popping up. It's because the beliefs are still right there attached to you and still being experienced *as if* they were true. The elephant and its limiting beliefs do not let go just because you have reached some goals, because it sits below the surface of your awareness, not above.

Shelly agreed that when she became successful, she thought she would feel differently about herself. But instead of escaping those feelings, the same insecurities and loneliness she always felt were still there. Except for now there was just more at stake.

Five Whys

NANCY ASKED FOR A volunteer to help her illustrate her next point. Roberta came forward.

Nancy asked Roberta what she'd learned so far in her journey about herself—her big why.

Roberta responded, "I've always wanted to use my gifts and talents to help empower others.

Nancy asked why.

Roberta said, "Because I always wanted to make a difference in the lives of others, especially kids."

Nancy asked why.

"Because I want to know that I made my name count in this world and that I had impact."

Again, Nancy asked why.

"Because I want to know I matter."

Nancy then asked, "So, if you were able to use your gifts and talents to help empower others, make a difference in their lives, leave a legacy, and know you made your name count in this world and that you mattered, *then* how would you *feel?*"

There was a long silence, so Nancy repeated the question. "So, if you were able to use your gifts and talents to help empower others, make a difference in their lives, leave a legacy, and know you made your name count in this world and that you mattered, *then* how would you *feel?*" As she fought back the tears, Roberta simply said, "I would feel . . . *good enough.*"

"Roberta, you thought all this time that you were moving toward living meaningfully with your rider, but deep beneath the surface your elephant does not believe you are enough. Your subconscious has a different agenda than what you are aspiring to. Your life is already pulling you in many directions above the surface, but what is also happening beneath the surface is further pulling at you and disconnecting you in ways you didn't even imagine.

In this fight between your elephant and your rider, your elephant is winning.

How We Cope

WHAT WE DO WHEN our elephant is winning is we find ways to hide. We hide in plain sight. We hide behind an image of what we have, who we know, what we wear, and our online image. We wear these like a coat of arms that shields us. We bury ourselves in our work and in what we do, and we are buried under all the things we do for others. We hide by filling our lives with the next social event, the next shopping trip, the next party, and all the ways we get around not being alone with ourselves and our thoughts. We hide by comparing ourselves to the people around us, even the ones we don't know. As long as we can tell ourselves that our lives are better than theirs, we can justify our disappointment. We tell ourselves it's too late, and we stay in the background of our own life. We stay busy so we no longer even think about the dreams we've deferred. We become resigned to the belief our goals are beyond our reach.

Choices or Concessions?

MARK ASKED, "WHAT'S WRONG with deciding to stop pursuing our dreams? Is making that choice so bad?

Nancy responded, "Let's think about it this way. When I walk into an ice cream store with lots of flavors and I pick one, it seems like I made a choice. But did I really? If I walk in that ice cream store and all of the flavors are truly available to me, I did make a choice. It is a choice because all the options are truly available and my decision came from all options available. But if I walk in the same store and only a few flavors are available because people like me are not supposed to eat some of the flavors, or I think others should decide what I eat, or if I have already decided I am not worthy enough to eat certain flavors, or that it's too risky to try some flavors even though I may really want to, then that is a concession. What appeared to be lots of choices early on quickly became very limited based on concessions."

A life of one concession after another without any real choices after a while can feel like you are living in a small, suffocating box. When you think you're just standing still and coping, the still, small voice inside you becomes a loud soul cry from within, and, as Ben Franklin said, it feels like you died at twenty-five but were not buried until seventy-five.

On most days, you may even manage to distract yourself from your dreams deferred. Except for this . . .

Dreams buried alive don't die.

So, in the still of the night, when your defenses are down, you look at your life and ask yourself if you are where you thought you would be. Did you put aside your deepest dreams based on the life compromises you made? Are you closing the gap each day between where you are and what you hoped you would accomplish in life?

In the quiet moments, what you know deep within you is that there is a profound pain, an emptiness that you can't outshake, outrun, or outfight because you know there is more inside you that you want and need to contribute, but you feel trapped in the life you've settled for. At night, you know you can't escape the sound of your clock ticking, and each morning, you wake up feeling *a little less* than you were the day before.

When Your Story Has You

As THEY SAT JUST taking it all in, Nancy asked, "Should I go on?" They all immediately said yes. She then asked if she could be more specific with each of them, and again, they all immediately said yes.

"When your story has you, there is something in your backpack you don't need. You're traveling too heavy, and it is weighing you down and holding you back.

"Shelly, you look like you've been on the fast track all this time because you've been chasing success, but the truth is, you've been sitting on the sidelines of your life. You're on the sidelines because you've adapted your life to other people's expectations. You've been sitting and waiting for someone else to tell you who you are, sitting and waiting for others to see in you what you refuse to see in yourself. And the more successful you become, the more at odds with yourself you feel." Nancy walked over to Shelly, who was seated, and said, "Shelley, it's time to get up. Get up and see the power you have right now, right where you stand, to rediscover your own truth. Let it live, and live *it*."

"Mark, you believe the sum total of your value and your worth is wrapped up in what you used to have. You don't believe your wife and family can ever love you without what you used to have because you don't love you without what you used to have. But the tighter you cling to that which you believe you need, the more you will continue to lose everything that really matters to you." Nancy went into his backpack and pulled an anchor from it. "Mark, let go of what you thought you needed in the past and see who and what you have always been without it—worthy."

"Gina, you're not sure you have what it takes. Despite all your fans, likes, followers, and people who believe in you, you don't really believe in yourself. You wrap yourself in lots of activity and a big image, but you've lost any real confidence that you can find and get what you really want. Your life is in constant motion, but all of that hides a deep fear that you won't be able to find your way home. You worry each day that everyone will see through your façade. You feel like an imposter in your own life. Gina, let me give you a mirror and allow you to see yourself for who you really are. Smart enough and capable enough—because you are enough."

"Bobby, you have big dreams, but you are playing small because your vision does not match who you really think you are. You don't really think you belong in the big leagues, so you talk yourself out of what you know. The minute you hit a roadblock, you back down because you've decided everyone is an expert but you. Everyone has something to offer but you. But the truth is they don't have what you have, and they can't see what you see." Nancy walked him over to a very big table with beautiful chairs all around it. "Bobby, have a seat at this big table, because you belong."

Nancy walked Roberta to a place where she could see an empty room and said, "Roberta, this room represents you. It's empty, just like you feel. You're empty because you stopped showing up on your own behalf a long time ago. So now your need to *please* others isn't just about how much you're doing for everyone else and how that's exhausting you. Your *need* to please is also about your *needing* others to stand in this gap, to stand inside this empty place and fill it *for* you, fill it *instead* of you. Roberta, it's time for you to show up, claim the real you, and fill that empty place in a way only you can."

Why You Are Stuck

Now speaking to the whole group, Nancy said, "Despite the pain and downward spirals, the pain is not what any of you fear. You don't fear, *despite* what you say, the self-sabotaging behaviors that leave you stuck. After all, this kind of slow death is not only familiar to you but also ultimately confirms what you believe about yourself—that you are unworthy. What you really fear is: Who would you be if you let go of what is most familiar to you? Who would you be without your story? That is what most frightens you."

Nancy then turned to them and told them it was time to let go of whatever did not serve them in their journey forward.

Every Beginning Begins with an End

AS THEY GOT BACK to land and disembarked from the boat, Nancy told them she had to take care of a few things and would meet them back at the cabin in a few hours so they should go ahead without her. As she gave them the car keys, Bobby asked if there was anything else they needed besides the keys.

Nancy said, "Everything you need, you already have." When they all got into the car, Nancy curiously added, "Every beginning begins with an end," which left them confused as they drove away.[5]

The route back to the cabin was one they were all very familiar with. But as they drove around, they got lost in their stories and eventually realized they didn't know where they were and they couldn't find their way back. They were lost for hours and eventually ran out of gas. They found themselves walking around in the wilderness, tired and confused. They had traveled too long, and their backpacks had now become too heavy to carry.

Just as night fell, they realized they were not alone. Since it was dark, they could not see clearly, but the sounds and the shadows in the distance were unmistakable. *Lions.* As they started to run away, they quickly realized they were surrounded on all sides and the *lions* were quickly closing in on them.

Now there was no way to escape, no place to run or hide. They were all afraid. Time was standing still. They felt as though they couldn't move forward because if they got too close, death was certain, but they couldn't turn back because there was no place left to go.

They each looked around for any weapon they believed could overtake and kill the *lions* from a distance, but they found nothing. They looked around for anything they could find to use as a weapon to defend themselves against the attack, but nothing worked. They were out of options but knew they had to stay and fight. In the midst of their fear and confusion, they knew that the only thing that mattered was staying in the here and now.

It was then that Bobby said, "Hey, let's think about what Nancy told us just before we drove off."

"Yeah," Gina said. Remember when she said, "Everything you need you already have." Mark said, "What if we don't need to build something to defeat these *lions*? What if it's something entirely different we need to do?"

"Maybe it's not something outside of us," Roberta said.

Shelly added, "Yeah, what if she meant we need to escape by letting go of the things we don't need?"

So, they took out of their backpacks the things weighing them down. They removed the things they did not need and kept only what they needed—the *Essential You* they uncovered days ago was all they needed to always keep and take with them no matter what circumstances they face.

It worked. The *lions* stopped charging. Now they asked each other how they could get rid of the *lions* altogether since they were still surrounded. Gina reminded everyone how Nancy had said, "Every beginning begins with an end." It was then that they looked at each other and smiled, because they got it. They knew what they had to do. And in that instant, they all yelled, "*The end.*"

And with that, the *lions* were gone. The travelers were able to walk and find life again. They were also able to refuel their tank and drive back to the cabins.

Defining Moments

WHEN YOU ARE HAVING a nightmare, you can do many things *within* the dream. You can run, scream, fight, hide, etc. None of these behaviors, though, can ever end the nightmare. The only way out of your dream state involves a change from dreaming to waking, because waking is not a part of your dream—it is an altogether different state.[6]

Similar to going from dreaming to waking in order to end a nightmare, ending the vicious cycle of the stuck lives so many of us live requires not just running, screaming, hiding, or fighting.

At some point, we will experience an event so devastating it throws our lives completely off course. We feel like life as we know it is over, and in some ways it is. It often includes needing to reinvent some part of our life. The key to defining moments is that they always bring you face-to-face with an opportunity to change the way you live, which means you will never be the same as before.

This requires you to change your paradigm to one that is outside your ceiling of limiting beliefs.

The reason the chaos and crisis that accompanies defining moments is so critical, though painful, is that you feel so overwhelmed and confused by what is happening. Because of this disorganization, you have no choice but to remove any resistance and live in the present moment in order to get through the crisis. You must detach yourself from the past and the limiting beliefs that kept you stuck in order to be present in the moment. Being in the here and now and surrendering to the confusion you feel allows you to break your frame of beliefs by bypassing your subconscious mind, interrupting your patterns, and dismantling the ceiling of beliefs that has been such a powerful force in your life. This allows you to look for solutions in places you never thought you would.

The End

WHEN THEY GOT BACK to the cabins, they told Nancy what happened.

They described the moment of finally winning against the *lions* as exhilarating since they'd defeated the *lions* and were finally free of what was weighing them down. It was also terrifying because now they didn't know what was next, so it felt like they were standing in a place of odd nothingness.

Nancy then said, "There comes a time in all our lives when we must come face-to-face with ourselves. It is a moment that forever defines us. You all were real heroes tonight."

And Then a Hero Comes Along

WE HEAR STORIES ALL the time of amazing rescues, of people finding a strength and power they never knew they had just when they needed it most.

Here's the thing about heroes: When a need arises, they act. That's it. They don't think. If they did, they would likely not act. They would talk or think themselves out of it. The immediate action is what breaks their frame of beliefs about what is and what is not possible.

They do this by focusing only on *right now*. They stay in the right now. There is no yesterday, no story of why they can't or shouldn't, just right now. Heroes disconnect from yesterday, what happened, and what it means. All that matters is what is happening right now. They disconnect from anything holding them back and act without any connection to anything they have "learned" or anything they falsely believed they needed.

The constant change and disruption that we are now experiencing in our lives often times feels like a crisis has hit us because of how quickly it comes upon us, and how quickly it forces us to decide what we should take with us and what to leave behind.

As a superhero, your strength, your superpower, lies in what you are willing to not be, not need, and not be defined by. Your superpower is in your ability to let go.

You can be a hero in your own life right now. You don't have to wait for a crisis to come upon you. You can always dial up the urgency in your life by creating a *right-now* environment that removes the things, people, and habits making it easy for you to just cope instead of move forward.

You will need to remove the things that serve no higher purpose and that just allow you to anesthetize and feel comfortable. Remove the things that are allowing you to sleepwalk through life.

Ultimately, the key is the meaning you make of whatever crisis comes your way. The key difference between those who just go from crisis to crisis and those who finally use them as a springboard for transformation is the meaning they are able to make of what has happened, which allows them to create a whole new mindset.

"So great," Roberta said. "How do we use this moment to springboard?"

Her fellow travelers said, "Yes, what do we do now?"

Nancy answered, "Tonight we get some rest and pick up where we left off tomorrow morning.

Stand in the Nothingness

THE NEXT MORNING, ALL the travelers received a surprise breakfast in their cabins instead of the common area, along with a note telling them to meet at the gym.

The outside of the gym was familiar to them. It was the outdoor course with the rock wall they climbed a couple days ago. Today, though, they went inside. As they went in, they had to walk through other rooms so that they could get to a special fitness room that was dead center of the building. Nancy explained that they were going inside instead of staying outside because the fitness they were building today was an inside job.

> Just as our body needs a strong core to provide the stability we need, we also must have a strong inner core to build the life-navigation skills we need.

Nancy said, "What is key in this period once you have let go of what is holding you back is aligning what your elephant believes with where your rider is going. We will do this by building up our inner core."

The travelers asked Nancy why this center room was so quiet.

Nancy explained that as they'd said last night, what they did in this time of exhilaration/odd nothingness was critical. It felt odd because the things they'd been using to prop themselves up, to feel comfortable while they hid in their life, were gone. Their old story was gone, but they hadn't built a new one yet since they hadn't yet learned how to build up the new fitness and habits so they could embrace their true *I Am*—their true inner core that should fill this room. "That's why right now," Nancy said, "it's like standing in a place of odd nothingness. It's quiet in this room so that you can finally begin to hear the sound of your own voice.

You now have to fill that nothingness with a new story about yourself, a new mindset, and form new habits. In this nothingness you are now learning to hear the internal feedback of your true voice, and your true self, where the other voices used to be. This nothingness is key because it is the space that opens you up to create a new story of who you are and fortifies your inner confidence. In other words, you are learning to become more centered.

This is crucial especially because when you walk forward in times of change and uncertainty, your internal compass needs to be what is front and center and leading you. A strong inner core will also help you create meaning and bounce back from even the most difficult situations so that you can persist and carry on no matter what.

"Ready travelers?"

"Yes!"

"Let's get started."

An Unshakeable Core

THE CRITICAL MISTAKE WE often make when we are in the nothingness is to spend way too much time thinking about and dissecting what brought us to where we are today. In other words, while insight into how we got to where we are is a really good thing, if we are not careful, we can end up spending all our time looking in the rearview mirror of our life rather than flooding ourselves with what we desire. Remember that we are already experts in what our elephant subconsciously believes about us, so we don't need to give that story any more oxygen or energy.

Instead, develop perfect eyesight for what you actually want. You have already removed the things in your environment that do not support where you are going. Now you need to spend time creating an environment that supports and reinforces what you actually want. This step is critical because what you focus on longest masters you, so make sure what you want is what is getting all your attention.

Breaking Old Habits

Now that you are trying to break the old habits that no longer serve you, your elephant will not give up easily. It will continue to sabotage you to keep everything as is instead of helping you move toward what you desire.

You've all experienced this at some point—the surge of fear that tends to show up just after you've had a moment of excitement when you realize you are moving closer to something you really want. Times like when you are exploring a sought-after new career, or you're ready to work on a new business you've dreamed of, or a move so you can take the next step toward what you want. This is when your elephant will flood you with self-doubt in double and triple force. That flood can at times feel overwhelming. It is in this moment that the negative self-talk will either shut you down, if you let it, or you can just steel yourself and refuse to let your elephant win. The muscle memory of your old, limited thinking will pull heavily during this time, so once again, you have to flood yourself with thoughts of what you want. Your elephant will do everything it can to stop you from changing and growing, especially since you're attempting to destroy the very story of who you are that you and everyone else has come to know as you.

Make a Different Choice

Now it's time to take it one step further and learn how to reduce the power your elephant has so that you can make sure your rider takes charge.[7]

Think back to what we said about your rider and elephant. Part of why your elephant is so powerful is that it is associational, and associations happen so much quicker than any rational, logical thought. So, when an event occurs, or someone says something to us, or we are faced with a new or ambiguous situation, our elephant has the upper hand because it will quickly *associate* the event with something familiar from our past, correct or not. Again, the key here is *without even thinking about it.*

Here's an example I'm sure we're all familiar with. We start taking a step that will move us toward what we really want. Then someone—our partner, a family member, or a friend—makes an offhanded comment that upsets us because it seems to confirm what our elephant is telling us. All of a sudden, we are thrown into a negative, downward spiral. The elephant has kicked in again because something someone said immediately resonated with what we were fighting our elephant about. It happens in an instant, and if we let it, we allow ourselves to ruminate about it for the rest of the day and it completely throws us off course.

What you need to do to stop that cycle is first, you have to cut the elephant and the downward cycle off at the pass. When you feel your emotions running away from you or the negative self-talk about to start, say, "*Stop!*"

The key though is don't just *say* "*Stop.*" You have to simultaneously *imagine* your rider—your superhero, looking directly at your elephant, who is charging at you, shouting "*Stop!*" In doing so, your superhero is powerfully keeping your elephant at bay. By shouting "*Stop!*", you are ending the immediate subconscious association that begins to happen even without your consent.

Next, say your name, followed by "Make a different choice." For example, if you're about to spin out based on what someone has said to you, you immediately say "*Stop!*", picturing your superhero, then you say, "(Fill in your name), make a different choice." You then insert a thought that moves you to where you are going; in other words, where your rider is taking you, rather than allowing yourself to loop into where your elephant wants you to go.

Saying, "Make a different choice," is critical because you must constantly remind yourself that it is indeed a *choice* to follow either your elephant or your rider. You must speak directly to your higher self and put your rider in charge by allowing yourself a moment to think about the direction you actually want to go, what you actually want to think, and the response you actually want to have that will best serve you.

Do this over and over again, as often as you need to. Visualize the hero in you becoming more and more powerful as you starve out the elephant in you. At first it will feel like a real battle; over time, though, you will realize that you can quickly cut the negative talk because your superhero has won the fight. Anytime the negative talk shows up to challenge the strong inner core you are building, strengthen your resolve by allowing your superhero to show up and come face-to-face with your elephant. Your superhero must always have the last word.

Making the Connection

JUST AS WE HAD to create a system of success by leveraging the power of networks and connections when we were learning how to make our outside plays, we now need to make sure we are creating the internal system of success we need to support ourselves internally. So that's why we need to make sure our mind-body-spirit connection is working for, not against us.

Our natural, biological response to change increases our stress levels, but we don't have to just be at the mercy of our stress reactions. Not only does exercise keep the body young, it keeps the mind vital and promotes emotional well-being.[8]

Regular exercise has the power to lower your stress levels and reduce feelings of depression and anxiety. Exercise causes the release of chemicals called endorphins into your bloodstream. These chemicals give you a feeling of happiness, which in turn positively affects your overall sense of well-being. Walking on a regular basis also promotes new connections between brain cells and staves off the usual withering of brain tissue that comes with age.

It's also important to be able to quiet your mind each day. In our world of constant chaos, without any way to regroup and find inner calm, mental overload and overwhelm can lead to anxiety and depression. Meditation is described as a state of restful awareness in which your body is resting deeply while your mind is awake though quiet. Regular, daily meditation is a powerful way to restore that inner balance and reduce stress. The travelers also visited the spiritual center that afternoon and talked about the importance of a strong inner spiritual life for each of them, regardless of how they choose to define and connect to their own spiritual center.

Stand Until You Know

IN THE MIDST OF constant change that sometimes requires us to let go of what has become so familiar to us, standing in the nothingness can be hard. It's hard because it feels like you are just standing in a space of emptiness. Sometimes you will hear nothing. It's odd because not only is there silence, but you will feel weightless because what used to anchor you is gone. In the meantime, you will want to go back and find something comfortable and familiar or someone to cling to. Don't.

Just stand in the nothingness until you can hear the sound of your own voice and you can tell yourself a new story about yourself. Stand in the nothingness until you know that your self-worth is not dependent on anything anyone has, says, or does, or on anything you can lose.

Stand until you know that no matter how many times people, life, and situations change, fade away, or even break your heart, you are able to say, "That is the end of that; it is not the end of me."

Nancy then told the travelers she had one more request of them: "Travelers, tell me who you are."

The greater the difference between the big vision of your life you are trying to get to and the limited belief of yourself that holds you back, know that you are in the fight of your life. Said another way, know that you are in a fight *for your life*.

Fight on.

The Beginning

Now the travelers saw a large board.

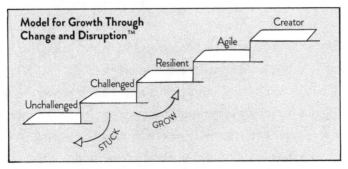

"This looks like where we've just been," Roberta says.

"It is," Nancy responds. "While we don't choose the chaos and disruptions that have now become a part of our backdrop, as you can see, this model emphasizes how you can grow despite change and disruption. This is the model that will help you go from stuck to resilient to agile, and then even to being a creator of your own future."

"As you can see at the first level, we are unchallenged. This was what it was like when we were sightseeing on our very first day here, and what it is like in the early years of our life. We take it all in, gain lots of experience, we feel good and confident, but we don't know or believe that it will ever change. For most, if you wait long enough though, you will arrive at the second level."

"This second level is where some challenge or change occurs, and this, of course, causes tension. But there are really only two choices: you can either try to stand still and cope, or you can grow. As we saw, many of us will at first just try to find a way to cope with disruption. But as we know, just coping, whether it's trying to stand in place and doing nothing, or trying to find some other way to lessen the pain, doesn't work so well. The problem is that there is no way to just stand still in life."

"When we think we're coping, we eventually realize we are walking ourselves in a downward spiral, and eventually we just become stuck."

"We've also learned how to use defining moments and the power of *right now* to let go of what is holding us back internally. This is what allowed us to break our frame of limiting beliefs."

"What we just learned in this indoor gym was how to grow by developing our inner core so we could be more resilient. Resilience is the ability to quickly and effectively recover from a challenging situation. The key to resilience is finding the growth opportunity that comes out of the challenge we are facing."

"But while resiliency is very important, we all came on this journey to do more than just bounce back. We came on this journey because we want to know how to thrive, how to make things happen, how to get to that holy grail of our life's sweet spot *in spite of* change and disruption, as well as how to be prepared for whatever circumstances we face."

"The next level on our journey today, is agility."

"Agility is what helps us anticipate what is ahead and not just react to challenging and changing situations. Agility is critical in being *FutureProofed* and is now a key part of how we have redefined being successful in our lives."

"Beyond agility, the final level is when we are not just responding to change but we become a creator of change itself. These are the people who are Wave Creators, who *create* new solutions to the big challenges they face so they can help not only themselves but also help others to find their way."

Nancy told the travelers, "Our next challenge today is figuring out how to go from being resilient to being agile."

Nancy took her travelers outside so they could walk around the building. This was when they noticed that not only was the indoor gym completely circular, there was glass all around it, so it was possible to have a complete view of what was happening on the outside from all around inside the gym. As they walked back inside the gym and around the rooms, they noticed that the fitness center was designed this way:

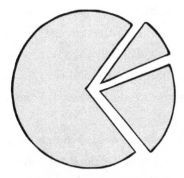

There were two smaller rooms and one very large room. The divider between the two smaller rooms was a glass wall, so that if you were standing in either of those two rooms, you could see what was happening inside the other small room as well as what was happening on the outside of the building.

The two walls that separated the two smaller rooms and the one larger one were not see-through, but there was a door on each wall you could open, allowing you to walk through it and see what was happening in that larger room if you chose. And because of its size, standing inside that large room and walking all around it gave you the best view of the three of what was happening on the outside, since it was the largest room. But the best view overall was if you accessed and walked through all the rooms to get a 360-degree view of what was happening outside.

Next Level

BACK WHEN WE EXPECTED to have one job or career for life, and our lives in general were more predictable and stable, our mental fitness was largely about having the resilience to bounce back from unexpected setbacks and stressors such as death, divorce, illness, job loss, or the financial problems we knew could knock us off our game.

But now that our careers are no longer seen through the lens of narrow career lanes, and now that change has become a way of life, mental fitness now means not only the ability to bounce back from setbacks when they occur but also the ability to spot new opportunities as they arise and being able to continuously look around for any potential challenges or risks.

These additional skills are needed so that regardless of what is happening or is about to happen it does not throw you off your game. Agility will let you move in ways that bring you peace of mind and constantly open you up to more choices, so it is key in being *FutureProofed*. While agility may have previously been considered a nice-to-have, there is no question that the mental fitness needed to become agile is now a need-to-have.

To be agile, we need:

- The first thing we need is a strong inner core. The unshakable core of *I Am* allows us to be resilient. As we built up our resilience in the fitness room at the center of this gym earlier today, we saw that our *I Am* is not only about identifying what makes us unique or valuable in the world like we did a couple days ago, but it is, at a much deeper level, also about knowing our own worth that is independent of external circumstances.
- The second thing we now need is to know how to develop the fitness so that we can not only see and spot *both* opportunities

and challenges, but we also must have the confidence, a strong *I Can*, to move through changing and uncertain circumstances.

Let's talk about how we are going to master the mental fitness we need to be agile so we can move around this outer ring of the gym.

THE AGILE MINDSET

THE FIRST KEY TO agility is a willingness to broaden what we see so that we are always maximizing our options. What that means is if we are able to move around and through each of these three rooms, not just one, we are much better off because we are able to see both opportunities as well as risks and challenges ahead and not just what is directly in front of us.

For this reason, the heart of the agile mindset is a both/and approach to navigating our environment. It is a mindset that allows us to embrace the fact that two things that may look like they are opposites and in conflict with one another, can actually both be true at the same time.

Seeing Both Problems and Opportunities

IN OTHER WORDS, YOU must be willing to see both potential opportunities and potential challenges; the things that can set you back, if you are going to get a 360-degree view of what is happening around you.

The power of both/and thinking is that it lifts you out of the either/or view we are used to—either just seeing the obstacles or just seeing the positives. When you are willing to see both, you can also begin to see more paths to opportunity in the midst of change and disruption than if your vision is limited to a more simplistic view of reality.

Beyond Positive Thinking

THE TRAVELERS AGREED THIS made sense, but felt it also seemed to go against the important concept of positive thinking. Nancy explained that they were right in that we often talk a lot about positive thinking and that overall, positive thinking is, of course, a good thing.

But sometimes we extoll the virtues of positive thinking to the point where we end up crowding out our ability to even see what is right in front of us. We filter out anything not considered positive. If we're committed to only seeing the positives and refuse to see what is right in front of us, it will constrict not just our way of thinking but also the way we act.

In fact, excessive optimism and excessive pessimism are just two sides of the same coin because in both cases, one to the exclusion of the other limits what we are able to see because we only have half a story. But if we allow ourselves to be open to the good, the bad, and the ugly as early as possible and not wait until it's too late to decisively act because we've limited what we see, then we are in a much better position to respond to changes when they do arise.

> *You can't solve a problem you're unwilling to have.*
> *—Bill Burnett and Dave Evans*

Here are examples you can probably identify with. Many times, when we are looking back at relationships that went wrong, we can identify that there were "red flags" early on that we chose not to really pay attention to because those flags did not fit with what we wanted to see. They did not fit with the view of what we were deeply committed to, so we just selected what information we viewed.

Or maybe we got bad news at work. The signs were there for a while, the handwriting on the wall was that there were going to be massive layoffs because things were not going well. We chose to not pay close attention and instead just stayed positive, until we and many others were told that massive layoffs were underway. Surprising? Not really, but now part of the anxiety we feel was because we now have fewer options available than we would have had if we had acted sooner.

The other side of this story, though, is the anger we feel toward our boss. We are angry because our boss only wanted to have "yes people" around him or her. The people who only gave the sunny side of what was happening in the company and blatantly ignored what was obvious to everyone else; that there was real trouble ahead. They all just kept affirming a rosy outlook on the world and acknowledged that anything else was happening only when it was too late.

The point is that we don't need to positive think ourselves into not seeing what is, because the fact is, we do face real challenges. The key is to see those challenges in ways that allow us to move around and through them with a confidence that says that we can ultimately prevail despite them.[9]

To do so, here is a second way those with an agile mindset think differently:

They See Themselves as Both an Expert and Beginner

PEOPLE WITH AN AGILE mindset can begin to move around and through challenges by embracing another both/and duality. But before I explain this duality, we need to talk about what is in these three rooms. These three rooms represent your three areas of knowledge.[10]

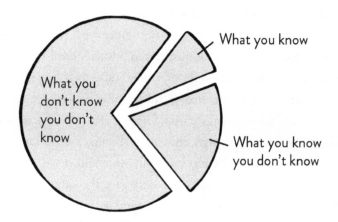

The first room here is "What you know." This is the room where we get rewarded for our expertise, or what we know, and it is where we live in our comfort zone. We build our confidence, usually just inside this room. For most people, our sense of *I Can* tends to come from this room because it rests on the inner confidence that comes from knowing your gifts, talents, strengths, skills, etc.

The room right next to it is "What you know you don't know." We tend to use this room selectively. The more we stay in the first room of what we know and it is working for us, the more we tend not to worry about this room, though we know it exists and we can see it and access it when we need to.

These are the two rooms that are accessible to us and to others just by standing and looking through the glass wall that divides them, because these two rooms are within the realm of what we know. But if we look carefully, the third, much larger room we cannot easily see through but can walk through the door if we open it, contains all the knowledge we don't know that we don't know.

Most of us stay completely out of this room.

This strategy of limiting ourselves to mainly what we know and se-lectively to only what we know we don't know worked for us when our lives were in a more steady state and was more predictable. When a big change happened, we could look out and round, and though we had a more limited view of what was outside of us, it was how we recovered from any setbacks.

But now, trying to just rely on that strategy is a dead-end path. Why? Because the vastness of the opportunities we will need to access in greater uncertainty lie in what you don't know you don't know.

So, when you root your sense of confidence, your *I Can*, from the view of only one room—only what you know, the expertise you are cur-rently rewarded for, and/or what is strictly within your comfort zone—your strategy also quickly becomes a limiter to your agility.

What people with an agile mindset do differently is develop their sense of confidence, their *I Can*, based not just on what they currently know, but on knowing that anything they do not currently know or currently can't do, they can figure out. They are defined both by what they know *and* what they *can* know.

In addition to what they know (their expertise), they also see them-selves as constantly being on a beginner's journey.[11] What I mean by a beginner's journey is a constant openness to learning new information and acting on it, even in high uncertainty, which takes them out of their comfort zone of knowing only what they know.

Both their expertise and beginner's journey of constantly seeking out and broadening their knowledge and experiences to help them as they continue to travel is what allows them to have a constant 360-degree view of their journey. Embracing both their expertise and being a beginner allows them to stay nimble and to expand what they see by opening the doors between the rooms and looking outside and all around them.

Now that we know that people with an agile mindset think differently, let's look at what they *do* differently and how they build habits that allow them to broaden what they see and move confidently even in uncertainty.

Building Habits for Agility

A Bias for Action

PEOPLE WITH AN AGILE mindset make a habit of getting out of their comfort zones by taking action. In order to take steps in times of uncertainty, they challenge what they think and what they know by taking action. They accept that they are not going to ever feel ready to act, so they must do things even when they don't feel ready. By simply starting wherever they are, they learn a lot more than if they just try to think their way through their journey.

They know that because most great opportunities in life sit outside the space of knowing what they know, they choose to stretch themselves and not just do what is familiar to them. They also do not just shut down because all of the next steps are not immediately clear.

Ask: How Can I?

WHEN THEY ARE LOOKING for solutions, and they don't immediately see them, they train themselves to ask, "How can I?"

Rather than just asking themselves *if* they can do something, adding the word *how* opens their thinking such that they always presume there is an answer or several answers. The *how* invites them to become more creative. The importance of the word *how* signals to them that an action or solution is possible. It signals them to look in other rooms by broadening their lens and stepping outside of what they know.

The word *how* underscores their ability to figure it out. How is not about confidence that they currently know all the answers or how to do all they will need to do. It is about the confidence that they can figure out how to find the answers. How emphasizes and empowers them to know they can figure it out.

They repeat these habits until it becomes automatic for them.

Shift, Not Drift

BOBBY ASKED NANCY WHAT was the difference in mental fitness between people who were agile and those just drifting along with no clear direction. Nancy said that question came up a lot. And here is the difference.

Drifting is when we have never occupied or we have left that center core room we talked about earlier. When we just follow whatever comes our way, whatever the next goal is, without any compass, no bigger why we aspire to or no inner center that grounds us. That is drifting.

Nancy grabbed a basketball and took the group to the basketball court. They were all familiar with the basics of the game, so as they played and passed the ball to one another, she told them to pay attention to how they played the game and to their footwork.

> **Pivot:** the action of stepping with one foot while keeping the other at its point of contact with the floor.

Once they'd played for a while, she asked them if they noticed how they were not just randomly running around the court. There was always a bigger goal—to make a basket. She asked if they noticed that they were never just aimlessly looking around. Instead they were always positioning themselves to either take a shot, make a play, or connect with the other people on their team so they could take advantage of passing opportunities to set up a shot. "Notice your footwork as well," she added. "Agile people, just like you all playing the game, stand in the center of a strong core and use pivot footwork as they look all around. One foot never leaves that center. It remains firmly planted. You used footwork to look all around so that you could take the shots you needed as the opportunity arose. This footwork is what allows agile people to spot opportunity in ways that are consistent with who they are, instead of just running all around the court or drifting.

"This mental fitness and footwork is what allows agile people to have peace of mind, regardless of what is happening around them, because they are always centered, and they are also always able to take the shots they need and to thrive because they can move forward and seek opportunity in a way that is consistent with their goals. So, unlike people who are just drifting based on what shows up at the moment, agile people, like you just demonstrated on the basketball court, are rooted in both their core and led by their compass."

The Power of Persistence

AGILE PEOPLE PERSIST BECAUSE they assume that as they move forward, they will be challenged. They assume they will face roadblocks, they will face circumstances where a solution does not seem clear, or face situations where they will fail repeatedly and feel discouraged.

They persist by actively seeking new information about what is happening around them and trying to sense and anticipate what may be coming. Their networks are critical in creating a continual feedback loop to challenge and expand what they see and know. They are always willing to expand their network so that they keep what they see and their information fresh. They learn from their failures, pick themselves up, and try again with new information, new skills, new techniques, and new angles.

Fear

PEOPLE WHO ARE AGILE have the right relationship with fear. They know that traveling to new heights and opening new doors will continue to kick up new doubts and fears. They know that just when they are ready to travel to higher altitudes, the journey will ask even more of them. As they keep traveling upward to new altitudes, they know it will get harder to breathe.

As they are stepping into new territory and climbing higher and they feel that twinge of fear, they see it as a good sign because it signals the progress they are making. In fact, fear is a sign they are on the right track. All of the fear they're kicking up is telling them they are playing at a level they are not used to playing.

They know that fear is also signaling to them that their elephant is wanting to pull them down to a lower level of belief and problem-solving rather than relying on their higher instincts. Unlike many other people, they do not try not to avoid fear, because they do not fear the fear.

So What? And Now What?

NANCY EXPLAINED THAT WHENEVER the fear kicked up, that was when we needed to imagine our superhero speaking to the fear and confidently saying "So what?" But here's the important next question: "And now what?" That is the important next question because we must follow that twinge of fear with *an action*. Don't allow fear to shut you down from acting; you must do something that moves you forward no matter how small the action is. For example, is it time to draft an email or place a phone call or reach out to a new contact? Again, the trick is *you must act.*

The Power of Leverage

JUST LIKE ANY OTHER skill, habit, or fitness you've learned so far, building mental fitness is not a one-and-done. You need to constantly build the mind-body-spirit connection. The more you develop your strength and endurance, habits, and footwork, the stronger you will be. The bigger your vision, the more agile you will need to be, as the journey will ask more of you. The more you work out, both on the inside and outside, the more you can leverage your mental, physical, and spiritual fitness and skills to work on your behalf.

128

HABIT FOUR

SUCCESS IS A LIFESTYLE, NOT A DESTINATION

⟨ THE TRAINS ARE RUNNING ⟩

THIS DAY STARTED OFF very differently for the travelers. Instead of meeting for an early-morning breakfast with time to chat and ease into the day, they got up much earlier than normal, ate a quick breakfast, and traveled to the nearby busy city. As they sat in the middle of rush-hour traffic, they took in the crowds, the traffic, and all the sights and sounds, which reminded them all too well of the hustle and bustle of their own daily lives.

While they were talking and trying to hear each other over the horns blowing and the above-ground trains passing, Shelly said she was surprised that their journey had brought them here because usually on retreats, the idea was to get away from the chaos, not travel into it. Everyone loudly and passionately agreed with Shelly.

"I brought you all here today, near the end of our journey together," Nancy explained, "because we all know how to take the time to step away from the hustle and bustle of our daily lives like you all have on this journey. We all know how to emerge from an experience like this feeling clear, excited, and confident about our direction. But the minute we go back home to our life, to our job, and to all our obligations, we are back to functioning on autopilot. Before we know it, we have lost the excitement, clarity, confidence, and the plot of our life once again.

"Today our journey is about learning how, even in the midst of the busyness of life and the world around us, to create a success *lifestyle* that will always keep our clocks and compass aligned. It is about learning how to always keep moving toward, and living in, our sweet spot."

Nancy explained that one big reason we often dread Monday mornings, especially after we've taken the time on the weekends to do things just for ourselves, is we know that when the alarm clock sounds, our life will quickly go back to a mode where the trains are all supposed to just run—fast and on time. It's all about time-telling. And for most of us, it is a pretty intricate dance on how to keep all those trains running on time. All of those must-dos from work and home wipe us out, and we are left feeling like we don't have the space to choose how to adjust those clocks in a way that keeps all the trains running but also in a way that better aligns with our own life compass.

Nancy pointed out that what they'd also learned early in their travels was that success is not a destination they'd get to only after doing a series of things sequentially or checking off a series of boxes. They'd learned that old path to success was on permanent detour. Instead, it is a lifestyle we need to build and choose each day.

If you ask most people about their sweet spot and the lifestyle they believe reflects what they want, they will say things like, "Make money," "Spend time with my friends and family," "Find happiness," "Have love in my life," "Achieve work goals," "Spend time on my hobbies," "Enjoy new places to see and experience," and "Know I am making a difference."

Clearly, there are a variety of things that define living in that sweet spot. But where it goes wrong for most of us is that instead of building a lifestyle that reflects a variety of the things we want, our lives end up being limited to just the few things required to keep those trains running on a daily basis. Much of what we *actually* want to do that would move us toward our sweet spot gets crowded out because of our daily must-dos.

Most people compare the kind of life we end up living to a hamster running on a wheel. It's a lifestyle with lots of action but where we're going nowhere and are stuck in the same spot. Another description often used is "living in the rat race." The rat race is when we spend our day working to pay the bills just to get up the following day to go to work to pay the bills. Yet once we have more money, but not more time, we just increase our spending to match the money. And then guess what? We just have a more expensive lifestyle; not more fulfillment, just more expenses. Only this time, we are even more trapped in the rat race because we need to work even harder just to pay the bills. Time passes quickly, and before we know it, we have lost sight of our sweet spot because we're stuck in a cycle of working just to pay the bills.

I think the comparison of life to a hamster on a wheel and rats in a race hits home in a way that is so visceral because when we feel like our lives have been reduced to this kind of daily chase with no enjoyment, we feel we have been stripped of something fundamentally human.

We are not created to merely exist; we are created to live.

—*Dr. Natalia Peart*

When you live in this daily race, where just one or a couple of aspects of your life completely consume you to the neglect of anything else, you move away from, instead of toward, your life's sweet spot. The result is long-term frustration and stress.

You want and need to be able to choose your lifestyle, the way you time-tell daily, in a way that allows you to align your clocks with your compass. What you *don't* want is to live like a hamster on a wheel in a life that's narrow, imbalanced, and disconnected from your compass.

Most respond to this imbalance with a quest for work-life balance. But that doesn't really work. Trying to achieve work-life balance is an attempt to fix a symptom with a one-size-fits-all solution of balancing work and life. It doesn't address the root cause of the problem. The problem is that you are not creating an *overall lifestyle* uniquely matched to your life's sweet spot.

Work-life balance isn't the answer because the problem isn't about balance. What you want is a more *integrated* life guided by your bigger life vision and compass—not just by the daily trains that run on automatic each day. Your integrated lifestyle must reflect what it means to live and feel at your best and highest. It takes deliberate effort; you can't just hope to arrive one day.

Next Level

THE KEY IDEA HERE is not just to divide your time and life, but to also effectively use your resources, time, energy, and attention to *integrate* your life as much as possible in a way that is most satisfying to you. Let's explore a few important steps that will help you build a success *lifestyle* and to *stay* in your sweet spot regardless of the busyness of your daily life.

YOUR LIFESTYLE LANGUAGE

THE FIRST STEP TO building an integrated success lifestyle is knowing your lifestyle language. Your lifestyle language helps you prioritize the areas of your life in such a way that you can optimize what you want to do and how you want to feel.

But before you do that, you will need to clarify one important thing for yourself. For most people, one of the biggest stressors in their life is the amount of space work occupies relative to everything else. You should therefore, get very clear about how much time you think work should occupy by asking yourself, "What does work even mean to me?"

For some, work is simply a job—a way to pay the bills, a means to an end. It is a way to fund the things they really love to do and the way in which they define their bigger vision. These people limit how involved they get with work activities and their coworkers because they want to maintain clear boundaries between work and all the other parts of their life. They want to get the job done, mostly for what their paycheck allows them to do *outside* of work.

For others, work is more than just a job. They want a career that provides them with a sense of accomplishment and likely the status and greater financial rewards that come with it. For these people, work is not simply a means to an end but often an important way for them to feel at their highest based on their performance. It's a way to get external praise and feedback for their achievements.

For others still, work is a critical aspect of how they derive their sense of purpose, meaning, and fulfillment. When they think about their bigger life vision, their work is a central part of how they define a meaningful life. For them, work occupies a different kind of space because what they want from it is central to their sense of fulfillment in life.

You need to consider what role you want your career to have and how much you believe that role blends with what you seek as your overall bigger life vision. Is your work just a job to fuel the other things you do? Is it a career that brings a sense of competence, mastery, and rewards for accomplishments? Or is it a vehicle for you to achieve your greater life vision?

Lifestyle Language Wheel

- **Impact**—A focus on your awareness of the world around you and your contribution to making a difference beyond yourself.
- **Personal and Spiritual Growth**—A focus on continual learning and growth and development of your spiritual life.
- **Love, Connection, and Belonging**—A focus on strong relationships with others, including your partner, family, friends, and close social and community connections.
- **Health and Physical Fitness**—A focus on overall health, including healthy eating, a healthy body, and healthy activities.
- **Financial Resources**—A focus on securing resources, largely financial, for your security and to meet your short- and long-term financial goals.

- **Work**—A focus on career aspirations and achievements and the sense of competence, mastery, and accomplishment your career can bring.
- **Fun, Hobbies, and Experiences**—A focus on the hobbies, sports, interests, experiences, adventures, and other ways you experience joy and happiness.
- **Creative Self-Expression**—A focus on your sense of creativity and uniqueness, whether in art, ideas, innovations, creations, or something else.

Rather than a quest for the one-size-fits-all work-life balance that has proven so elusive, let's instead begin by discovering your more nuanced lifestyle language. Your lifestyle language is a tool that I often use to understand the relative priority of the different aspects of your life that define what you are really after.

To quickly see your areas of priority, rank the items on this wheel in order of importance to you. Now look at your top five. These are generally your lifestyle language must-haves. These tend to be voids that you feel *most deeply* when they are absent from your life, and they are *most critical* to you living in your life sweet spot.

As you consider your areas of greatest importance, ask yourself:

- Do these lifestyle language priorities incorporate both my compass and my clocks?
- Do my lifestyle language priorities represent the synergy I must have between me at my highest (my life compass) and how I want to spend my time on a daily basis?
- Do my lifestyle language priorities help me create a lifestyle that compels me to reach higher, deeper, and further each day? This is because the pursuit itself must make you feel alive and vibrant right now, not just at some imagined destination in the future.

- Does my lifestyle language optimize my being with my doing and my bigger vision for myself?

Now look at the items that were not in your top five. They are likely things you still want, but they may feel more to you like nice-to-haves instead of must-haves in your lifestyle language at this point. In other words, it would be nice if you could get those things, but you won't feel deep pain if they are missing.

To check to see if your lifestyle is currently a good geographic match for you, think about other factors such as:

- Do you prefer big or small towns?
- What is your ideal weather?
- Do you prefer rural, suburban, or more urban cultural environments?
- Are different kinds of educational opportunities (creative/innovative or intellectual) important to you?
- Do you prefer a more active lifestyle?
- How important is community and sense of belonging to you?
- Do you have faith-based preferences that you should make sure to keep in mind?

Once you've ranked what you ideally want your lifestyle language to be, look and see what your lifestyle language is right now.

Now ask yourself:

Is my current lifestyle at all reflective of my desired lifestyle language? Is it close to what I ideally want?

The gaps you've identified help you see what areas you should start making a priority, especially if there is an area that is important to you but is completely absent in your current lifestyle language.

At different points in your life, you may emphasize different areas over others, just as you need to constantly update your career portfolio based on feedback about the plays you make. In the same way, you need to keep track of your lifestyle language and update it as needed so you can stay in your sweet spot.

Now that you know your lifestyle language and any gaps that exist, let's learn a few ways to help you build the lifestyle you want.

Leverage Support

THE TRAINS ARE ALREADY running in your life, but if these areas are really a priority for you, you need to make it harder for these priorities to get squeezed out of your life. You need to build in accountability for what is important to you. To do that, look for or create support systems for different aspects of your lifestyle language so you don't continue to crowd out the things that are important to you. Are there groups, communities, or circles of people, whether online or in person, that you know or that you can join that share your motivations and direction such as the GetFutureProofed.com online community?

At this point, some of the travelers experienced a moment of shock when they realized just how far off they were from living their desired lifestyle language. Second, they began to think about how busy (not full) their life is right now. They started to think and talk about how hard it was to keep the trains in their life running right now, so they could not imagine where and how they would squeeze anything else into their life.

Let's talk about that. How are you going to shift your time, attention, energy, and resources to create the lifestyle you want? Before we even begin to build a new set of habits that you will need to make the changes you want, let's clear up a few misconceptions right now.

Misconception #1

Multitasking—When the Solution Becomes the Problem

Nancy next said, "Okay, travelers, here is a question for you. With a show of hands, how many of you consider yourself a good multitasker?" All hands went up immediately.

She continued. "A big issue for those of us with an ever-growing list of demands on our time is how to manage it all when time is a finite resource. We constantly try to find ways to tackle the problem of too many demands on our limited time. The problem is so bad that it's to the point that multitasking has become a way of life for most of us. Just about everyone does it, and we wear it like a badge of honor because it somehow seems to convey that in this fast-paced world, we are not only able to handle more than others, but we are also being more productive than others.

If you're a multitasker, you probably think you are solving your time-crunch and productivity problems. But here are a few misconceptions about multitasking that may surprise you.

When More Is More

There are times when multitasking is a good thing. It works well when the two tasks you are doing at the same time use *different* parts of your brain. When that happens, the tasks complement, not compete, with one another.[1]

For example, taking a shower often sparks very creative thoughts. Those two tasks don't compete with one another. Instead, they seem to help each other. Another example is using long walks or other forms of exercise to increase your creativity. Again, those kinds of tasks are not using the same part of the brain, so they complement one another. Walking and other kinds of exercise help change your brain chemistry because your heart pumps faster, circulating more blood and oxygen to all your organs, including your brain.

Where Multitasking Breaks Down

YOUR MIND CAN ONLY effectively focus on one task of the same type at a time.[2] Here's what that means: despite what you think, you're not good at doing two things that require the same cognitive brain attention at the same time. For example, you can't be good at sending emails while talking on the phone. Studies have shown that adding tasks that tax the brain in the same way causes performance on each task to deteriorate— meaning it will not only take longer, but you won't be as accurate. And once you have been distracted from the original task, it takes the brain as long as fifteen minutes to refocus.

Are You Even Multitasking?

IF YOUR BRAIN NEEDS to constantly refocus when distracted from one task, are you really even multitasking when you say you are? Dr. Jim Taylor[3] says that although people think they are multitasking, they are actually serial tasking. He defines serial tasking as "shifting from one task to another in rapid succession." When you say you're multitasking by writing an email and talking on the phone at the same time, for example, what you're really doing is typing part of an email, then stopping and switching to your phone conversation, then stopping and returning to your email, and so on.

When More Is Less

THE FRENETIC SERIAL TASKING of your life is not making you more efficient or more productive. It's quite the opposite, and it's even worse than you know. Here's why:

"Multitasking" (or, more accurately, serial tasking) not only lowers productivity by 40 percent, but your long-term memory and creativity can also be reduced.[4] And this doesn't even address the mental exhaustion it produces.

The cycle we are finding ourselves in with constant serial tasking is that you do this for a while, but find you are not being productive enough. Then you look to more tools to help you become even more productive, because you're convinced you just need to squeeze more in with less time. That leads to burnout. Only then do you realize it's time to recharge—largely because you have no choice. Once you recharge, you quickly find yourself back in the burnout cycle again—wash, rinse, and repeat.

It's a Series of Sprints, Not a Marathon

RATHER THAN WAITING FOR burnout to hit again, a much better way to think about being more productive is to see it as a series of sprints, not a marathon. Tony Schwartz of the Energy Project[5] says that in order to operate at your best, you need to renew your energy at ninety-minute intervals—not just physically but mentally. He cites the discovery of pioneering sleep researcher Nathan Kleitman, who more than fifty years ago discovered something he called the "basic rest-activity cycle." As Kleitman describes it, there are ninety-minute periods at night during which we move progressively through the five stages of sleep, from light to deep, and then out again. This cycle, called the ultradian rhythm, is present in both our sleeping and waking lives.

Your brain can focus for only 90 to 120 minutes before it needs a break. That is why when you need to rest, your body sends you clear signals such as fidgeting, hunger, drowsiness, and loss of focus. Many of us just ignore these signals and treat the symptoms with things like loading up on caffeine or simple sugars for a boost. The problem is that we then become addicted to the adrenalin rush because we never fix the real problem—we just treat the symptom.

Schwartz recommends that it is far better to take breaks after these 90- to 120-minute cycles for higher and more sustainable performance. You will be more productive if, at the end of these cycles, you take a few minutes to step away and disengage from mentally challenging tasks, giving your brain time to rest and recover.

Misconception #2

The Battle for Our Energy

YOU, LIKE EVERYONE ELSE, are being constantly pushed and pulled in too many directions. We've already talked about the competition for our time and how to create a lifestyle language that allows us to prioritize that time. We've also talked about the constant battle to be more productive and how it is better to single task with renewal breaks. Now let's talk about the battle for our energy.

When you discovered your lifestyle language, spelling out the way you ideally want to spend your time, you were better able to see ways to *productively* use your time. Those are not however, the only ways you use your time throughout the day. Aside from the *lifestyle activities* that are more purposeful and are generally intended to move you toward and keep you in your sweet spot, there are also *maintenance activities*.

Maintenance activities are things like daily chores, cleaning, errands, commute time, cooking, cleaning, repairs, coordinating kids' schedules, shopping, and the other things you do to maintain your life. *Passive activities* are ways you kill time and zone out completely, like using social media and watching TV. Finally, *restorative activities* are the things you do for your own well-being, such as reading, exercising, yoga, spending time alone, resting, and relaxing.

You can't create more time, but one way to make sure you can move toward and stay in the sweet spot of your life is to find ways to *optimize your energy* and to *expand time.*

What does it mean to expand time?

We saw earlier how a crisis in your life that takes all your attention can feel like it stops time altogether. When time "stops" and you are forced to stay in the right now, you can use that time stop to your advantage because it helps you break your frame of beliefs. Now, let's go to the other extreme, where you are in a state of flow. You are so completely engaged in an activity and so completely in the zone it seems you have expanded time. That sense of being so deeply absorbed in your experience, so fully engaged, is what also allows you to lose track of time completely. You can also leverage the energy you create from these deep experiences to restore the energy reservoir that is often depleted in your quest to keep all the trains running.

Ideally, you want to maximize the amount of time you spend on things that increase your vibrancy and aliveness, optimize your energy, and expand your time as you minimize those things that are draining you.

To create energy and a sense of being alive, you need to first determine where you are leaking energy more quickly than you can create it. In other words, you need to start by identifying the big energy drains on your lifestyle. That means paying close attention to whether your environment at work, at home, among your friends, and in other areas is helping you expand your energy or drain it.

One very big opportunity you have for generating more positive emotions and increasing your energy each day is doing work that matters to you. If you are working in a way that is consistent with what is meaningful and feels effortless, you will feel like you are expanding time.

Within the different areas of your lifestyle language, you spend so much of your time at work, but it drains energy far more often that it boosts energy. One shocking statistic from Gallup makes this clear.[6] About two-thirds of American workers are "not engaged" or are "actively disengaged," meaning they are emotionally disconnected from their workplace and are less likely to feel or be productive. That leaves about one-third of workers who are "engaged," or involved in and enthusiastic about their work. What's worse is that this level of disengagement has remained high for years. Here's the conundrum: for most people, our work life engages a small part of us yet asks so much of us, all at the same time. We stay because we need the paycheck. We stay because we are scared. But when we count the cost of staying in these energy-draining situations, we must also consider the emotional toll these job mismatches take on us.

Another way you drain energy is through routine maintenance activities. These are the activities that must be done, and the coordination that must happen, for you to keep the trains running. There isn't good news about maintenance activities, either. Between our long and hectic commutes, planning our kids' schedules, maintaining our household, and on and on, it is tough, stressful, and overwhelming to manage our very complicated lives.

We are always looking for ways to lessen the maintenance load that drains our life. Whether it is negotiating better ways to share the household responsibilities with our partner or seeking work environments that are more flexible, there are no easy answers on how to best reduce the drain. Even if we can't eliminate them, we should try to minimize them as much as we can.

If you think about it, it should not be surprising at all that most of us are struggling to keep up with all of the daily demands placed on our lives now. Aside from the high level of coordination that is required to walk the tightrope each day, if we just look at the changes in how we work, we see that we now must create a career playbook with multiple plays that we can run (sometimes at the same time) to hedge against risk, and help ensure we can always move forward despite what is happening around us. What this means though, is that our work life can now be considerably more fragmented than it was in the past. Toss into the mix the concerns that we previously discussed when we were putting together a more fragmented work life such as health insurance and saving for retirement, it often feels like there is little room for error.

Let's shift for a moment and take a look at our environment and how it contributes to more stress, burnout, and anxiety. We are overwhelmed by the fast pace of not just our life but of everything around us. Most people are worn out by the dizzying amount of news we are flooded with each day. We are addicted to our phones—with 24/7 connectivity, we are now constantly interrupting what we are doing to check what's happening online. Not to mention the constant comparisons we are making of our own lives to perfect social-media-ready lives and images. We often feel like we come up short. Even unread emails can serve as huge distractions to us.

But it is not just the fact that it is a lot of news, it is also the onslaught of negative news now coming to us on a twenty-four-hour news cycle. Not only do we continue to read about the daily violence and shootings that plague our communities (if it bleeds, it leads), we are now dealing with crises, like more school shootings, mass shootings, terrorism, climate change; and more natural disasters, like hurricanes, floods, wildfires and tornadoes, than ever before. This is all within the context of a highly divided and polarized nation. When you put all this together, it is more than enough to keep us in a state of hyperarousal—a prolonged period where we feel like we are living in crisis mode. And this is all before we have even factored in our own daily stressors and strains.

None of this is good for our health. Anxiety disorders are now the most common mental-health condition in the United States, affecting forty million adults age eighteen and older, or 18.1 percent of the nation's population each year.[7] And it's quickly getting worse, even among college students. The American College Health Association found in its annual survey that in 2011, half of undergraduates reported they felt "overwhelming anxiety." By 2017, that had increased to 61 percent.[8]

That's why restorative activities like physical exercise, mindfulness, and other ways to strengthen your mind, body, and spirit are so critical. Let's look for a minute at mindfulness:

> **Mindfulness** is the self-regulation of our attention with an attitude of curiosity, openness, and acceptance.

As a practice, mindfulness emphasizes purposely paying attention and keeping that attention focused on the present moment. It's an important counterbalance to the routinized way of functioning just to keep our day-to-day tasks running. It requires you to be in the here and now.

Shifting or Drifting?

THERE IS YET ANOTHER battle for our energy that we don't often consider. If you think about our lifestyle language in a way that is similar to the way we thought about our predictable patterns, then you will see that our lifestyle language is also the blueprint for how we most naturally want to draw energy from, and stay engaged in our life on a day to day basis. When we stray too far from our lifestyle language in order to meet the immediate demands of everything else competing for our time and attention, we find that over time we are no longer just briefly shifting from our language, but we have completely drifted away from it.

We no longer even try to prioritize what is meaningful and effortless to us, or that builds or restores our energy, because now we are on a downward slope. It feels like too much work to figure out how to reconfigure a very complicated life by trying to stop the momentum and walk upward. Before we know it, we are moving pretty quickly toward being stuck in a rut.

Just as we learned on our first journey that there is a right and a wrong way to find our big picture vision, there is also a right and wrong way to shift our time, attention, energy, and resources to create the lifestyle we want. The wrong way is what we normally do, especially at particular times like the start of the year. We declare big resolutions in January of each year after taking stock of our lives, but by February, 80% of us have already broken those resolutions. There are a number of reasons why resolutions fail, not the least of which is the fact that when we make those resolutions, we have not put in place the right systems for momentum or leverage, nor are we utilizing a few key principles that are critical to how we change our behavior.

Change is a process not an event

—Barbara Johnson

Now, let's learn the seven key steps we all need to know (especially if you are stuck in a rut), to shift from where you are right now to your ideal lifestyle.

Step One: Visualize Where You are Going

- Our first step is to create before-and-after visual maps so you can clearly see what you need to do and how to best prioritize all the different activities on your list so you can create the lifestyle you want.

LIFESTYLE MAP™

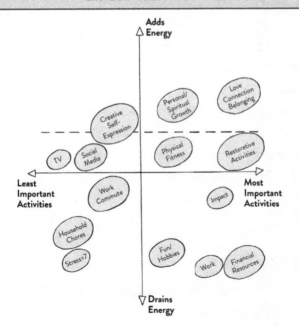

As you can see, you are going to map the things you don't really care about too much across the horizontal line (x axis) on the left. These are the things that are less important or not important at all to you. Now map the things you really care about on the axis all the way to the right. These are the most important things in your life.

On the vertical line (the y axis), you are going to put at the top the things that feed your energy. Moving to the bottom, you are going to map the things that drain your energy.

Notice there are also two areas in the dotted lines. The left side consists of the things you are doing that just waste your time. On the right are the things you need to start doing because you want to incorporate them into your lifestyle and/or they have the potential to increase your energy.

For Your Before Map:

To CREATE YOUR MAP of what your life looks like right now, take your list of must-haves for your lifestyle and fill those in first. Now fill in your nice-to-haves. Finally, add your maintenance, restorative, and passive activities.

Make sure you are filling in the most important activities to the far right. As you move left, fill in those that are less important.

Anything toward the bottom means that is really draining you.

Finally, think about your stress level and give it a number between one and ten. If it is a five or above, put that number in the lower-left quadrant.

For Your After Map:

Now START BY LOOKING at where you want each of the lifestyle activities most important to you to be. You should be starting from the far right and working left, because those are most important to you. Anything on your *before* map that is a lifestyle priority to you, yet is in the lower-right quadrant, should be a priority to work on because it is important to you, yet it is a drain and not satisfying you right now. This should represent what you ideally want to spend your time improving.

The sample map above shows that this person needs to prioritize their restorative activities. She is looking at a career change because she is unhappy in her current job, so that is also a priority in her lifestyle language, just as fun and recreation are. Weekly household maintenance chores are depleting her energy. She is also wasting a lot of time just zoning out. Her stress score of seven brings attention to the fact that she immediately needs to do something to disrupt her current pattern of living.

Now that you have your visual representation, this is how we will continue the process of shifting our behavior to create the lifestyle we want.

Step Two: Gain some momentum for your journey

- Check to see if your stress score is too high
- Decide if you should prioritize a few restorative activities even before beginning on other parts of the lifestyle map, as any change you intend to make, whether you see it as positive or negative, does require you to use some emotional and time resources. Do you need to build up your reservoir?
- Consider getting some inspiration and support for the journey by joining the GetFutureProofed.com community.

Step Three: What you are willing to let go of, in order to free up time and resources

- What should you stop entirely?
- Can you remove time wasters—time you're spending just zoning out completely on things like social media and watching TV?
- Can you outsource or renegotiate things that are truly exhausting you in the short run (these are likely the things in the lower-left quadrant)?

As you think about the things that are exhausting you, keep in mind that your predictable patterns apply here as well. If you are not a detail-oriented person, but much of your life has now become managing lots of details, that will take a huge emotional toll in ways that you are not likely considering.

Step Four: Use the power of leverage and enlist a team of people to help you create your system for success

- Are there people who excel in areas where you need extra support that can be part of your team to help you manage some of the activities?
- Can you barter time and services so that you can be of mutual benefit?

Step Five: With some momentum and a team of support in place:

- What are you going to start doing?
- What priorities will you shift? Are you spending too much time on things that don't ultimately matter as much?

Step Six: Adjust your expectations

- One reason that people give up when trying to make changes is that they believe that once they have decided to make the changes, the hardest part is done. That is not the case. Keep in mind that starting new endeavors will require huge adjustments which in the short run can be an energy drain. This is where you need to put into practice all that you have learned about yourself, and the power of leverage along our journey in order to go from before to after.

Step Seven: Celebrate small successes along the way

- Do not just wait for many big changes to celebrate progress. Build a daily habit of celebrating some progress, some victory, however small it may be.

With these seven steps, now continue to fill in the rest of your map and activities to go from your *before,* to *after* in a way that creates a visual guide for you to shift in the way that you would like.

When you look at your *after* map, it should represent:

- The highest of what you really care about.
- The highest of feeling fully engaged in your life.
- The optimization of your passions, interests, and sense of joy.
- The peace of mind your map will also help you reduce stress, anxiety, and a sense of vulnerability.

Your Lifestyle Map™ should help you create the lifestyle that enables the integration of your doing and well-being—a lifestyle that enables you to thrive and bring your *full self* to each day.

Additionally, your change process for moving toward your desired lifestyle, should also encourage your overall career, financial, lifestyle, mental, and physical fitness.

⟨ Are you *FutureProofed*? ⟩

OVER TIME, WE ALL have learned to value not just dieting to lose weight but instead living a healthy, active lifestyle. We have also learned to value not just how much we make, but also being financially fit through paying down debt, having a savings and retirement account, etc. Today, I believe it is just as important to think about whether we are not only physically or financially fit, but whether we are *Futureproofed*. When we look at our overall career, financial, life, mental, and physical fitness, we should be asking ourselves where do we fall on critical questions such as:

Career Fitness:
- Someone else is fully in control of my career vs. I am in control of my career.
- I am job hopping vs. I have my own career playbook.

Financial Fitness:
- I have no emergency fund vs. I can weather a storm.
- I live paycheck to paycheck vs. I am able to fund and support my dreams.

Lifestyle Fitness:
- I am not living my lifestyle priorities vs. I am living my ideal lifestyle.
- I am in a rut vs. I can shift as necessary.

Mental Fitness:
- I am stuck vs. I have an agile mindset.

- I do not see a future vs. I am the creator of my future.

Physical Fitness:
- I am in poor physical health vs. I am in great physical health.
- I live a sedentary lifestyle vs. I live an active lifestyle.

These are just a few questions to give you an idea of what it means to be *FutureProofed*. To take the full quiz and get your profile, visit GetFutureProofed.com.

Your Well-Being

WHEN CONSIDERING YOUR WELL-BEING, a good way to think about it is the PERMA model designed by Dr. Martin Seligman.[9] You will notice that I have modified the model to also include what we all now look for in response to our constantly changing world—peace of mind.

Well-Being

P: Peace of mind frees you of the anxiety and strain of a constantly changing or uncertain environment so you can thrive.

P: Positive emotions fuel you on a day-to-day basis and help you feel good.

E: You are engaged in your life; time stands still, you have moments of flow, and you are living at your highest.

R: Your relationships are authentic connections.

M: You have a sense of meaning and a purposeful existence.

A: You have a sense of accomplishment in your life.

THE SIGNAL IN THE NOISE

FINALLY, HERE IS ONE more tool to keep you clear and focused on your *after* map, even when the Monday morning trains of life start running.

Days ago, when we learned how to go from managing our job to managing our playbook, we needed a portfolio—a tool to help us track our plays and the feedback that we get from each of them—in order to help keep us moving in the right direction.

It's the same thing here. We need a way to track our plays so we can always separate the signal from the noise.

The problem with most traditional calendars is that they focus on day-to-day productivity, not on the big picture of your sweet spot or the lifestyle you need to get there. On the other hand, most journals allow you to express your compass goals, but too often these goals end up poorly tracked on a regular basis.

What you need is a planner system that picks up where your lifestyle map leaves off.

Nancy provided each of her travelers with a planner system that allowed them to translate their lifestyle map in a way that tracked their progress, optimized their living in the now as well as for the future (in other words, it's both compass-and clocks-focused).

It's the same kind of planner system you need. It pulls all of the aspects of your life together so you can see the day-to-day tasks as well as the long-term goals so you are always able to see your end game.

There is yearly, quarterly, and monthly goal tracking of your success markers so you never lose sight of your compass, a view of how to look at your week and translate your time spent based on your life map, and quick reminders on how to build important habits on a daily basis.

As Nancy's travelers became immersed in their lifestyle maps and planners, they realized it was time for them to return to their cabins. On the way back, they again got caught in rush-hour traffic—this time the evening traffic—and they again watched the passing trains and heard the loud honking of horns. But this time they spent their time with their new planner systems, using their maps and laying out their plans for creating the lifestyles they really wanted.

They took turns sharing their plans with one another. They told Nancy that even though the journey was not over yet, they felt ready and excited for the dreaded "Monday morning."

They reported that what they'd learned that day was that taking time away from their normal lives allowed them to break away from the trains that ran in their lives—the automatic, rote ways they were currently living their lives. They realized that the key was to find a way to create a strong system all around them, from their lifestyle language to their lifestyle map, from their communities of support to all the tools and resources that would help them form new habits and make a deliberate choice each day.

REACHING FOR THE SKY

⟨ COMING FULL CIRCLE ⟩

O
N THEIR LAST DAY, the travelers met for their usual morning chat and found out they would be ending their travels in the same way they began: walking the very road they had the first day so they could reflect on all they had learned.

As they started out, Nancy said, "When I think back to our first day—to our very first conversation about what brought you here and what you each wanted—it was clear you represent the many people who know it's time to take this journey. You represent those who are exhausted by, and lost in, the busyness of their lives. You represent those who feel unsettled in their lives because they don't yet seem to know their direction. You represent those whose lives used to make sense but no longer do and who need to figure out what the next chapter brings. You represent those who used to be successful but who had to start again. You represent those who faced disappointment and are now resigned to a small idea of what their life could be. And you represent those who *seem* to be successful but feel every bit as trapped as they did when they were struggling to make it. You were all looking to invent or reinvent yourselves in these unpredictable times, and you came because you wanted to know what it would take to be successful in today's world.

"We set the stage that this was not going to be a typical journey. To get to where you each wanted to be, we could no longer play by the rules of success that we were used to since the world has changed. All the disruptive technology and our more globalized, networked world means we live in a time of constant change and greater uncertainty. The world of work has changed, as we've seen the death of the job for life and the rise of the freelance economy and more independent ways working. And what we want from the world has changed because, ultimately, we want to merge both personal fulfillment and professional success in ways that allow us to feel more integrated, and we want the peace of mind that comes with knowing that regardless of whatever storm comes, we will be able to find our way back."

As Nancy finished, the travelers arrived at the new path of success and *FutureProofing* they'd found the first day—the path they'd taken to get to the beautiful mountains in the distance. Nancy challenged them to consider the rules they had learned along the way.

Habit One

GINA RECALLED THEIR FIRST adventure when they learned the new destination of success and *FutureProofing*. They found the path that blurred the bounds between how they worked, lived, and played, and with it the peace of mind that came from knowing they were equipped with the new skills they needed in a constantly changing world. She then talked about flying over the mountains and looking for the moments that mattered and the patterns that gave their compass a magnetic quality so each of them could unfilter their lives and begin to discover their compass and clocks.

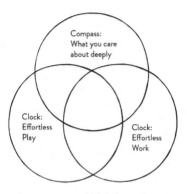

Habit Two

SHELLY REMEMBERED THEIR SECOND day—and with it the big shift in perspective they needed to make from just thinking about getting the next job to learning a strategy for having more choices and more control over their lives. They learned to take charge by being the boss of their life, creating their own success markers, and discovering their "essential you" and "unique advantage." She remembered how they also learned key work-navigation skills, like creating their playbook, prototyping, acting in the face of uncertainty, getting feedback, and telling their own story.

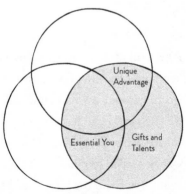

Habit Three

Roberta said that on the next day of the journey, they learned that the skills needed for getting to and living in the sweet spot were not just work skills—they also required life-navigation skills. She added that what was different about these times was that constant change and the stress and anxiety it caused were now part of the backdrop of their lives. That made it critical to have a strong, unshakeable inner core of *I Am*.

Mark pointed out how they'd learned agility is key in being *Future-Proofed*, in spotting new opportunities as they arise, and in being able to continuously look around for any potential challenges or risks. He demonstrated the pivot footwork to keep their inner core strong and to constantly look around for opportunities they might not know existed.

Habit Four

Bobby wrapped up by reminding them that success is a lifestyle, not a destination. He talked about learning how to break out of the constant busyness that leads us to run our lives on automatic so we can move to living the lifestyle we choose. He added that they discovered their life-style language, visualized what they wanted through their maps, and learned the key steps they needed to know to shift to how they used their time, energy and attention to build the integrated lifestyles they wanted.

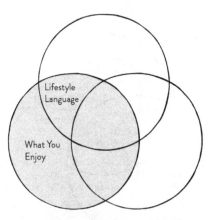

As the group arrived at the beautiful mountains they'd seen that first day, Nancy said, "Great job, travelers. As you look to your sweet spot—in other words, the peak of your mountain—this is where your human being and human doing come together."

She explained that one more takeaway from their time together was that they didn't need to spend time searching for their life purpose; they just need to start where they are and begin with what they care about. They just need to get in the game, pay attention to what they choose, what they trade, what they fight for, and what does not let go of them. In other words, finding their purpose was about recognizing the patterns of their *lived* experience.

"You can create the meaningful life you want inside your sweet spot," Nancy said, "as long as you don't filter your journey—as long as you keep your compass in sight and stay agile so that you are always able to be *FutureProofed* and open to new opportunities. Your purpose will find *you* as long as you commit to living your life *unfiltered* and bringing your *full self* to the journey. Sometimes it unfolds over time, and sometimes it suddenly finds and grabs ahold of you."

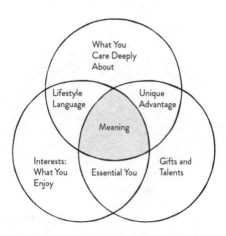

LOOKING BEYOND THE MOUNTAINS

As THE TRAVELERS FINISHED looking at the mountains and reflecting on their journey, Nancy asked them to look up beyond the mountains to the skies instead of looking down at the mountains from the skies like they did their first day. "As you look to the skies," she said, "I want to talk about the last level of mental fitness beyond the agility we mentioned a few days ago. This is called the *creator level*. At this level, you don't just respond to change, you become a creator of change itself."

"Travelers, this is what the final level is all about. If you recall, people with an agile mindset can take a 360-degree view of problems and opportunities because in addition to having a strong inner core that keeps them firmly grounded, they are very comfortable navigating the three rooms of knowledge. Those three rooms, as you recall, are "What You know," "What you know you don't know," and "What you don't know you don't know."

As a creator, you are not only comfortable navigating these three spaces, you also take another, very different journey. Your journey is different because you know that when you look for a 360-degree view of opportunities, you are still looking *within* the boundaries—the silos, assumptions, and limits that define your current circumstance.

> *We cannot solve problems at the same level in which they are experienced.*
>
> —*Albert Einstein*

As a creator, you seek higher ground and search for different solutions entirely by looking up and *lifting out* of the silos and the thinking that created your current circumstance.

You don't just accept the rules, laws, and assumptions that have come to define what you "know." You don't add to what you "know" by simply looking around your current environment. Instead, you disrupt the status quo by breaking the frame and assumptions of *what* you know and *how* you have come to know what you "know." You break bounds by looking up and out beyond the boundaries and constraints that have come to define what we all just accept as givens, enabling you to see things from a completely fresh perspective.

Creators are in all industries and sectors, all places and spaces, and they come from all walks of life. The ways in which they channel their gifts and talents in the world are as varied as they are, but at their core, they all do three things:

One: They Look Back but Vision Forward

CREATORS USE THE PAST to inform what they do, but they are not anchored in the past—they are forward looking. They are neither constrained by the past nor bound by the limits or chaos of the moment. Instead, they use their knowledge of the past to help find ways to transcend their current reality in order to create the future.

Two: They Refuse

CREATORS REFUSE TO SIMPLY meet the world where it is. They refuse to accept problems as they are. They refuse to just adapt to what they see when they look around. And they refuse to give tacit consent to the constraints that give rise to the reality of their today.

Three: They Create Transformative Solutions

SINCE THEY ARE NEITHER anchored to the past nor constrained by the present, creators aim for more than incremental improvement from what they see today. Their goal is not change. They seek *transformation*, which is about creating something entirely new instead of simply a better version of what they see. They address root causes rather than the symptoms of problems.

⟨ Reaching for the Sky ⟩

NANCY LET THE TRAVELERS know that she wanted to shine a light on a specific group of creators. She wanted to talk for a moment about those for whom their own success is just the beginning, not the end. For them, learning to effectively navigate the new world is critical but not enough. Their vision compels them to look beyond their own success because what they are ultimately seeking, is societal impact. They want to break down the barriers in the current ways of thinking and operating so they can help others around them.

These creators look to transcend the boundaries and limits that have created such steep and unsteady climbs to success for so many in these chaotic times. They look up and ask, "Why is the journey this way?" "Why is the water around us so choppy?" "What are the assumptions we must all question?"

*Where you stand determines the problems and solutions
you see.*

—Chris McGoff

Defining Moments

NANCY ASKED THE TRAVELERS, "Why am I mentioning these specific creators to you? Why does all of this matter *right now*?" She then explained, "It matters because we are living in a pivotal moment in history. It is a time that will define us for decades to come. When we look at the state of the world today, on the one hand, rapid innovation and globalization have transformed the way we work, live, and play, bringing with them both opportunities and challenges. The world has changed, the world of work has changed, and what we want from the world has changed. These shifts have left a huge gap between where we are today and how we as individuals and as a nation must adapt. The turbulence, the widening gaps, the pain and unrest we see, all challenge us to bring forth new solutions.

But the thing about defining moments is that whenever there are periods of major challenge like this one, a new generation of creators always emerges to help break down old boundaries and ways of thinking and operating. They bridge the gap between where we are today and where we need to be in order to help us all cross the divide to living more successful, meaningful, and *FutureProofed* lives.

How Might We?

TRUE CREATORS KNOW THAT they alone cannot solve complex, "wicked" societal problems—that is the fallacy of one. True creators are instead *catalysts* who vision forward. They create big, hairy, audacious goals (BHAGS)[1] that inspire others to be part of creating a new future. They are catalysts because they know that solving large, complex, and sweeping societal problems is not just in the domain of some—those with certain titles or in certain sectors and spaces.

They disrupt the status quo *even further* by bringing people of all talents, skills, and perspectives together to help solve tough problems because they know that when we are all looking up to the sky from diverse angles, backgrounds, and experiences, and we are bringing our diverse talents and skills, that is when we can get the clearest, most *unfiltered* view of the vastness of the blue sky and all its possibilities.

True creators don't just ask *How can I?* they reimagine the possibilities for new solutions by asking *How might we?*[2]

The travelers again looked up and basked in the blue sky and all its possibilities. It was the perfect ending to their journey together. As evening began to fall, they all went back to their cabins to relax, pack, and get ready to travel home early the next morning. They decided that after packing they would meet in their usual group-chat spot one last time.

When they got back to their cabins, there was a folded piece of paper under each of their doors. They all assumed it was the final bill. Instead, it was a note that read:

> The cost of this journey has been paid for
> by someone else.

One by one, each went to the front desk to ask who had paid for his or her journey, but no one at the desk knew anything about the notes. When they all met again, the first question they asked each other was about the mysterious note.

They were all left feeling confused. They sat and repeated over and over, "Someone else paid the cost. Someone else paid the cost. Someone else paid the cost." They didn't get it . . . until they did.

Instead of the light chat they had originally intended to have, they spent the next several hours in deep discussion. They were inspired. They were the most excited they had been in a long while. They felt alive. Time flew by quickly, and when they were done, they called Nancy to meet with them one final time before they all left.

They told her about the notes and how they finally got it. What they understood was that they were the beneficiaries of all the people who'd come before them. They were the beneficiaries of all the people who, rather than just living in the chaos and challenges of their time, also saw what could be. They understood that they were the beneficiaries of those who, when challenged, felt compelled to stand in the gap and take bold action so that they could live in a better world—and help *leave* a better world for everyone else who came after them.

The travelers now saw the journey they had taken together as a way for each of them to journey to their own mountains peaks *and* to look to the sky so they could create new paths for others. They called on Nancy one more time so they could present their new BHAG—a goal so audacious it inspired them to keep working together after they left. They wanted to use the gift this journey had been to them to not only *move forward* in their own lives, but also to *pay it forward*.

> *The best way to predict the future is to create it.*
> —*Peter Drucker*

Here is what the travelers told Nancy about their discussion. As creators:

One: They Look Back but Vision Forward

THEY LOOKED ACROSS TIME and saw that while we are fortunate to be living in a time of great opportunity, there are some pain points that over time *have pervasively and often disproportionately* impacted us and *changed our overall odds* for success. They were clear about saying *overall odds* because they were looking on the whole and, in the aggregate, not just at each of them and us as individuals.

They looked for a few big trends that told them that while there was lots of progress and opportunity, there were also challenges large enough to keep people from bringing their full selves to travel their full journey. These challenges matter because, on the whole, they limit our ability to fully participate in our own lives and the world around us, which in turn limits our ability as a nation to reach our full potential.

For example:

1. Across generations, we have had to adjust how we think about being upwardly mobile based on our income. According to Harvard University economist Raj Chetty, if you were born in the 1940s or 1950s, you were virtually guaranteed the American dream of earning more than your parents did. But that's not the case anymore. While the rates of upward mobility were 90 percent for kids born in 1940—meaning that 90 percent of those kids went on to earn more than their parents—that figure has steadily declined to 50 percent for kids born in 1984. "For kids turning thirty today, who were born in the mid-1980s, only 50 percent of them go on to earn more than their parents did. *It's a coin flip as to whether you are now going to achieve the American dream,*" Chetty says.[3]

2. The real wages of most workers in the United States have barely budged in decades. Despite a strong labor market, wage growth has not met expectations. In fact, today's real average wage (that is, the wage after accounting for inflation) has about the same purchasing power it did forty years ago.[4] And because of rising inequality, whatever wage gains there have been have mostly flowed to the highest-paid tier of workers.[5] When we take into account the rapid growth in the cost of health care, it is no surprise that the cost of health insurance is cited as a major stressor for two-thirds of American adults.[6]

3. Looking at more generational trends, Baby Boomers and Gen Xers were able to work their way through college and graduate with little to no debt. This is almost impossible for Millennials. Student loans now make up the largest chunk of non-housing debt in the nation—more than both credit-card and auto-loan debt.[7] The huge disconnect between the rising costs of education and wages that have not kept pace makes it harder for graduates to launch their lives while paying back student loans.

4. **Preparation Matters.** Our educational system has always played a central role in helping us develop our full selves so we can fully participate in the world around us. The problem though, is that twentieth-century education no longer prepares us for life success in the twenty-first century, so students now are routinely graduating without the twenty-first-century skills needed to succeed.[8]

5. **Place Matters.** When it comes to our ability to not only be fully prepared but to also travel our full journey, our zip codes—

the places we grow up—are a powerful determinant of our upward trajectory. Not only does economic mobility vary widely across our nation, it varies, significantly, right down to city and county levels.[9]

6. **Participation Matters.** Nothing is more fundamental to who we are as a nation than being able to go as far as our talent and hard work will take us. Yet, according to McKinsey & Company and Lean In,[10] despite significant gains in degree attainment, corporate America has made very little progress in improving the full participation of women and people of color at all levels of leadership and decision-making. Women and people of color are also significantly underrepresented in Silicon Valley. According to the Case Foundation,[11] we "aren't tapping the full potential of America's innovation and ingenuity" because when you consider venture capital, only 10 percent of venture-backed companies had a female founder; only 1 percent had an African-American founder. And when it comes to venture capital, 78 percent of all venture capital in the nation goes to just three states: California, New York, and Massachusetts, leaving the other forty-seven states to share just a quarter of the pie.

Two: As Creators, They Refuse

THE TRAVELERS SAID THAT in the same way *inner* limiting beliefs create resistance to developing our full selves, *external* limiting beliefs create points of resistance that limit our full journey and full participation. But they refuse to accept the limiting beliefs that permeate so much of how we operate—such as the belief that for some to win, others must lose. They don't believe that success must be a zero-sum game where we must fight over a shrinking pie and the winner takes all. They believe that in these chaotic times, we can all find higher ground through mutually beneficial actions that expand the pie itself.

To make that happen, they believe it is time we tell ourselves a new story about ourselves. It must be a new story that relies on our higher instincts as a nation.

They believe that if we all help create the ecosystem that helps us bring our full selves, travel our full journey, and fully participate in our lives and the world around us, we can all reach not only our own full potential but also the full potential of our nation.

Three: A Transformative Solution

Success is an Ecosystem

THE TRAVELERS TOLD NANCY that they want to work together to create a new national education/preparation-to-success ecosystem that helps us all bring our full selves to travel our full journey, and that encourages full participation at all levels of leadership, decision-making and innovation in our nation.

They know that not only do we need our educational skills to keep pace in our twenty-first-century economy, we also need the work-and life-navigation skills for success. We must also focus on consistently updating ourselves so we can be *FutureProofed*.

Preparation is no longer just about what happens in the classroom, nor is it just the domain of educators and the school system. It is now about exposure to the experiences, connections, people, and things that *open* opportunity and *reduce* barriers through strong networks, role models, advocates, and sponsors for our journey. What this means is that we must be all in—we need to bring all sectors, industries, and people who want to contribute whatever they can, wherever they can, and however they can to building not just their own success but to building our education/preparation-to-success ecosystem.

The travelers know that we can all achieve this BHAG if we see ourselves differently. We need to see ourselves not just as people who can successfully thrive in the midst of change but *also* as people who can create change—and therefore *create* the future. We need to see ourselves as people who are all part of a larger educational/preparation-to-success ecosystem. If we see our own success as a beginning and not an end, and we are willing to ask *How might we?*, we can all reach for the sky and help lift others as well. For the travelers, then, this journey is about looking to the mountains *and* the sky.

The travelers each went to sleep that night excited for the next chapter. Their journey was not coming to an end just because it was time to go home. In fact, it was just beginning.

Wherever your journey leads *you*, our world is waiting for you to bring what you have to offer.

THE BEGINNING

NEXT STEPS

I hope you have enjoyed reading about the journey of these five travelers and that you're inspired to begin your own journey to being *FutureProofed*.

Go to **GetFutureProofed.com** and take the Get *FutureProofed* challenge.

- Discover your *FutureProofed* Fitness by taking the Are *FutureProofed*? quiz.
- Receive information and inspiration for your journey based on your goals.
- Join a community of people taking back control of their lives, charting their own course, and building an inspired new future.

ACKNOWLEDGMENTS

THIS BOOK HAS TRULY been the journey of a lifetime, and to everyone who has been a part of making this happen, I am deeply grateful.

Thank you to my parents, who have always believed in and supported me. You gave me the confidence to reach for the sky and never give up. You have been there when I needed you most. I could not have asked for more.

Brandon, this is for you. You are truly my gift. To my brother, Michael, and my entire family—thank you for putting up with all the sacrifices it took to finally bring this book forth—you all have been my rock.

Thank you to Angela Eschler for your insight, inspiration, and partnership. Thank you to Christopher Bigelow, Michelle Nelson, and Kathryn Jenkins. Thank you to my chief editor, Michele Preisendorf. I truly appreciate not just your expertise, but I thank you for your enthusiasm for the book and the message. Thank you to Melissa Dalton for your marketing wisdom and all of your support that helped bring my vision to life.

Thank you to Dayna Linton for your interior design, your true commitment, partnership, and willingness to jump in the trenches to make sure we made it all happen is something I will never forget.

Thank you to my very talented cover designers, Zeljka Kojic and Mitch Chandler for your visions and partnerships.

To my very patient friends who have all been so supportive and have waited for me to get my life back, a huge thank-you. You've always been in my heart, and I've missed you all more than you can ever imagine.

Finally, I am forever indebted to all of the amazing mentors, teachers, and guides throughout my life, some who know me and some who don't, but you have all helped show me the way.

"I am because we are."

NOTES

Habit 1

1. Abraham Maslow, "A Theory of Human Motivation," *Psychological Review* 50, no. 4 (1943): 370–96.
2. Stephen Covey, A. Roger Merrill, and Rebecca R. Merrill, *First Things First: To Live, to Love, to Learn, to Leave a Legacy* (New York: Simon and Schuster, 1994).
3. Mihaly Csikszentmihalyi, *Flow: The Psychology of Optimal Experience* (New York: Harper & Row, 1990).

Habit 2

1. Bureau of Labor Statistics, U.S. Department of Labor, "Employee Turnover in 2018," September 20, 2018.
2. More resources for self-assessment can be found at GetFutureProofed.com.
3. John Holland, *Making Vocational Choices: A Theory of Careers* (Englewood Cliffs: Prentice-Hall, 1973).
4. Bruce Reed and Matthew Atwell, "The Rise of the Expert Economy: Could Sharing Wisdom Be the Next Gig?" *Civic,* 2018.
5. Bankrate, "37 Percent Have a Side Hustle," *Bankrate,* June 25, 2018, https://www.bankrate.com/pdfs/pr/20180625-side-hustles.pdf.
6. Tim Brown, "Design Thinking," *Harvard Business Review,* June 2008. https://hbr.org/2008/06/design-thinking

Habit 3

1. Jonathan Haidt, *The Happiness Hypothesis: Finding Modern Truth in Ancient Wisdom* (New York: Basic Books, 2006).
2. George Pratt and Peter Lambrou, *Code to Joy: The Four-Step Solution to Unlocking Your Natural State of Happiness* (New York: Harper Collins, 2012).

3. Benedict Carey, "Who's Minding the Mind?" *New York Times,* July 31, 2007.

4. Science Daily, "Neuroscientists Identify How Trauma Triggers Long-lasting Memories In The Brain," August 18, 2005, https://www.sciencedaily.com/releases/2005/08/050814175315.htm.

5. See William Bridges, *Transitions: Making Sense of Life's Changes* (Boston: Addison-Wesley, 1980).

6. Paul Watzlawick, John Weakland, and Richard Fisch, *Change: Principles of Problem Formation and Problem Resolution* (New York: Norton & Company, 1974).

7. Thomas W. Lombardo and Samuel M. Turner, "Thought-Stopping in the Control of Obsessive Ruminations," *Behavior Modification* 3, no. 2 (1979), 267–72.

8. Mandy Oaklander, "How to Bounce Back," *Time,* 2018.

9. Jim Collins, *Good to Great: Why Some Companies Make the Leap . . . and Others Don't* (New York: Harper Business, 2001).

10. Joseph Luft and Ingham Harrington, "The Johari Window, a Graphic Model of Interpersonal Awareness," *Proceedings of the Western Training Laboratory in Group Development,* 1955.

11. Stanford Design School, "Beginners Mind," https://dschool-old.stanford.edu/groups/k12/wiki/4e22d/Beginners_mind.html.

Habit 4

1. Jim Stone, "The 7 Laws of Multitasking: The Two Main Hazards (and Two Main Benefits) of Multitasking," *Psychology Today,* December 16, 2014.

2. Jim Taylor, "Technology: Myth of Multitasking: Is Multitasking Really More Efficient?" *Psychology Today,* March 30, 2011.

3. Ibid.

4. Paul Atchley, "You Can't Multitask, So Stop Trying," *Harvard Business Review,* December 21, 2010.

5. Tony Schwartz, "A 90-Minute Plan for Personal Effectiveness," *Harvard Business Review,* January 24, 2011.

6. Amy Adkins, "Majority of U.S. Employees Not Engaged Despite Gains in 2014," *Gallup*, January 28, 2015, https://news.gallup.com/poll/181289/majority-employees-not-engaged-despite-gains-2014.aspx.

7. Anxiety and Depression Association of America, https://adaa.org/about-adaa/press-room/facts-statistics.

8. Katie Reilly, "Record Numbers of College Students Are Seeking Treatment for Depression and Anxiety—But Schools Can't Keep Up," *Time*, March 19, 2018.

9. Martin Seligman, *Flourish: A Visionary New Understanding of Happiness and Well-being* (New York: Simon and Schuster, 2011).

Habit 5

1. James Collins and Jerry Porras, *Built to Last: Successful Habits of Visionary Companies* (New York: Harper Business, 1994).

2. Stanford Design School, "'How Might We' Questions," https://dschool-old.stanford.edu/sandbox/groups/dstudio/wiki/2fced/attachments/f63e8/How-Might-We-Questions-Method.pdf?sessionID=a4c32167e58dc598ac57b770de7cb0f4f838ac50.

3. Raj Chetty, John Friedman, Nathaniel Hendren, Maggie R. Jones, and Sonya Porter. Working Paper. "The Opportunity Atlas: Mapping the Childhood Roots of Social Mobility," September 2018.

4. Drew Desilver, "For Most U.S. Workers, Real Wages Have Barely Budged in Decades," *Pew Research Center,* August 7, 2018, http://www.pewresearch.org/fact-tank/2018/08/07/for-most-us-workers-real-wages-have-barely-budged-for-decades/.

5. Ibid.

6. APA, "Stress About Health Insurance Costs Reported by Majority of Americans, APA Stress in America™ Survey Reveals," *American Psychological Association*, January 24, 2018, https://www.apa.org/news/press/releases/2018/01/insurance-costs.aspx.

7. Emmie Martin, "Here's How Much More Expensive It Is for You to Go to College Than It Was for Your Parents," *CNBC Make It*, November 29, 2017, https://www.cnbc.com/2017/11/29/how-much-college-tuition-has-increased-from-1988-to-2018.html.

8. U.S. Chamber Foundation, "Bridging the Soft Skills Gap: How the Business and Education Sectors Are Partnering to Prepare Students for the 21st Century Workforce," *U.S. Chamber of Commerce Foundation*, 2018, https://www.uschamberfoundation.org/sites/default/files/Closing%20the%20Soft%20Skills%20Gap.pdf.

9. Raj Chetty, Nathaniel Hendren, Patrick Kline, and Emmanuel Saez, "Where Is the Land of Opportunity?: The Geography of Intergenerational Mobility in the United States," *Quarterly Journal of Economics* 129, no. 4 (2014) 1553–1623.

10. Women in the Workplace 2018. *Leanin.org and McKinsey & Company*, 2018, https://womenintheworkplace.com/.

11. Inclusive Entrepreneurship, *Case Foundation*, https://casefoundation.org/program/inclusive-entrepreneurship/.

ABOUT THE AUTHOR

D R. NATALIA PEART IS a Psychologist who has spent more than 25 years as a leading expert in helping people and organizations navigate change to achieve business and personal success. In her various roles as a clinical psychologist, a leadership and performance consultant for national Fortune 1000 companies, a leader of nonprofit organizations and as an executive and personal consultant, she has always been driven by a desire to help solve tough problems.

She earned her B.A. with Honors in Psychology from Brown University, her PhD. in Clinical/Community Psychology from the University of Maryland, and completed her Clinical Internship at Harvard Medical School.

Dr. Natalia is the Founder of the Catalyst Innovation Group, LLC, a company devoted to helping people and organizations change successfully. She has served on the Federal Reserve Board, 10th District, and has been featured in various media outlets.

CPSIA information can be obtained
at www.ICGtesting.com
Printed in the USA
FSHW011619121219
65009FS